MADE TO CHANGE

MADE TO CHANGE

HOW TO POSITIVELY DISRUPT YOUR LIFE

REBECCA BEAGAN

NEW DEGREE PRESS
COPYRIGHT © 2020 REBECCA BEAGAN
All rights reserved.

MADE TO CHANGE
How to Positively Disrupt Your Life

ISBN
978-1-64137-559-7   *Paperback*
978-1-64137-560-3   *Kindle Ebook*
978-1-64137-561-0   *Digital Ebook*

Dedicated to my grandmother, Blanche Kennedy, who taught me the meaning of love and the value of perseverance. My Mamaw, you cared for me growing up, and we needed each other after your father and husband went to heaven and my parents worked for the family. Thank you for your shining example of finding your identity in Christ, staying positive, and pouring your heart into nurturing your family. You are my sunshine, always.

CONTENTS

	INTRODUCTION	11
PART 1	**ALCHEMY**	**21**
CHAPTER 1	WANDERING THE DESERT	23
CHAPTER 2	VISION AND PURPOSE	37
PART 2	**STORIES OF CHANGE**	**49**
CHAPTER 3	WHEN VISION GOES WRONG	51
CHAPTER 4	WHEN LACK OF VISION GOES RIGHT	65
CHAPTER 5	WHEN VISION EMERGES	81
PART 3	**WRITING YOUR VERSE**	**99**
CHAPTER 6	RESOLVING VISION	101
CHAPTER 7	FRAMEWORKS AND PRACTICES FOR THE GROUP	113
CHAPTER 8	FRAMEWORKS FOR THE INDIVIDUAL	125
CHAPTER 9	TECHNIQUES TO RESET EXPLORATION	143
CHAPTER 10	ETHICS AND VISION	153
CHAPTER 11	CONCLUSION	161
CHAPTER 12	MY STORY OF CHANGE	169
	ACKNOWLEDGMENTS	189
	RESOURCES	191
	APPENDIX	193

> "*When I fall, I shall rise; when I sit in darkness, the Lord will be a light to me.*"
>
> —MICAH 7:8 ESV

INTRODUCTION

"Hey, I just bought a fifty-dollar student ticket to Harvard Business School's Private Equity and Venture Capital Annual Conference. It's the weekend after next. Want to go?" Leon, my boyfriend and fellow classmate at Chicago Booth Business School, asked as he turned around in his swivel desk chair.

This is not unusual for Leon. He is truly a free spirit—spontaneous and lighthearted, curious and whimsical. Even sitting there in his swivel chair, his desk lamp on, bare feet, shorts, and t-shirt in January, his Bose headphones giving him a beat to nod his head to, *The Office* playing on his television—this free spirit is looking up conferences to attend, marathons to run, and flights to take.

Being a bit more of a planner but giggling to myself, I quickly pulled up Kayak.com and checked the flight prices—not bad. So, not thinking too much more about it, I said, "Sure, why not. I haven't been to Boston since before B-school. It'll be fun." I quickly found the registration link and purchased my student ticket, too. We were booked.

Having worked in management consulting before graduate school and attending Chicago Booth at that time, I knew what the private equity and venture capital industries were, but I never saw myself going into these fields for a career. Still, I am a fairly curious person and many of the breakout sessions related to hot topics and trends in industries in which I do have interest.

As a type-A planner, I considered what I wanted to get out of going to the conference. My primary goal in going to the conference was to learn a bit more about these industries since I have worked with clients in them in consulting (my pre- and post-Booth career), gain insights into how they are thinking about hot topics in my areas of interest, and have good food and good fun with Leon and friends attending the conference in Boston.

* * *

"Welcome to Boston. It is now safe to use your hand-held mobile devices...." the flight attendant said as we landed in Boston the Friday night before the conference. Sleepily, I exited airplane mode. 12:05 a.m. We had to take a late flight because we had a book writer meeting the evening before.

Leon and I were both in a program for students with a couple other people at the University of Chicago. Each of us in our small group was working on writing our own books. I was a bit annoyed that our book writer meeting was scheduled for Fridays at 5:00 p.m. It was our third group meeting since launching our writing group in January, and I was still the only one without a topic for my book. Earlier that week, my writing coach, Professor Eric Koester from Georgetown University, founder of Creator Institute, asked me to take the pressure off a bit and think more about whom I wanted to learn from and what I wanted to learn more about. Grabbing my suitcase from the overhead bin, these thoughts about what my topic would be lingered in the back of my mind.

Being familiar with the hotel scene after many consulting travel weeks spent in Boston, I chose something familiar and comfortable, not wanting to chance it with an AirBnB or a hotel I didn't know. Yes, I came to Boston on a whim for a conference that was not directly pertinent to me, but I could at least plan what I wanted to get out of the weekend and sleep somewhere I had stayed plenty of times before. I am a planner, after all.

* * *

BEEP BEEP BEEP BEEP.

6:00 a.m. Groggily, I turned off my alarm. I wanted to make certain we had enough time to get across one of the bridges in Boston to get to the conference in Cambridge. We also didn't know the layout of Harvard Business School very well, so I wanted to budget plenty of time so we weren't late. Again, not unusual for me, but not Leon's approach. Regardless, we made it.

After a day filled with speakers and panels, from artificial intelligence to healthcare and more, the last session was coming up. It was a keynote session with a venture capitalist.

It was about 4:00 or 5:00 p.m. "Do you want to stay for the keynote?" I asked.

"Sure, we might as well stay," Leon said.

So we grabbed a row in Harvard Business School's large auditorium. From the stage set-up, it was going to be a moderated session, with one facilitating interviewer and the keynote speaker. I opened the conference booklet to read about the speaker: Ann Miura-Ko, founding partner of Floodgate, a venture capital firm. I scanned the write-up: "...early investor in Lyft, TaskRabbit, Refinery29, and companies in machine intelligence..."

I was intrigued. A quick Google search showed "the most powerful woman in startups," according to Forbes. Gosh, I thought, what a statement. I bet she had life all figured out from day one.

Then they walked out on stage, Ann smiling cordially and taking her seat by the interviewer on stage. After an introduction and a couple of warm-up questions by the interviewer, Ann was asked, and I'm paraphrasing: "Ann, you clearly have made incredible accomplishments and have a variety of experiences. You are now described as 'the most powerful woman in startups.' Can you tell us how you got here? What was your vision? How did you plan for such great success?"

And Ann's response, paraphrasing: "I didn't. Actually, my life was rather emergent."

My jaw dropped. I felt Leon look at me, and jaw slack, I looked at him. I knew what he was thinking. Emergent. It was a word I had been playing with the past couple of weeks. I was taking a class at Booth focused on leadership and personal strategy and just had a course section on emergent strategy, the idea that sometimes personal or even company strategy emerges when current dynamics require more flexibility.

In probably what were seconds, I had flashes of conversations and scenes from the past years and months come to mind that seemed to point to this idea of life being "emergent":

- Four years as a management consultant with most of my work helping companies with corporate strategy, exploring vision and advising on strategy
- A business leader mentorship program session about writing my purpose statement
- A conversation with fellow classmates about whether they had wasted opportunity at Booth by going into the fields they are entering, not knowing ultimately where it will lead, and what they want to do with their lives
- Discussions in the leadership and strategy class at Booth about "the journey" and "emergent strategy"

And now, Ann's statement: "Actually, my life was rather emergent."

It was then that I knew my book topic. I wanted to write about purpose and vision. But not in the traditional sense. I didn't want to tell my audience how to discover their purpose or articulate a vision.

People may think successful people are the ones who planned it all out: they create a career plan and they follow it. After all, we are asked from a young age by well-meaning parents and relatives what we want to be when we grow up, hoping that asking us will prompt thought and help us pick a direction that will result in success.

In this book, I want to highlight what I've learned: that often, the most successful people are not the ones who have everything figured out from day one. Rather, they are the ones who learn how to become emergent; they learn to be flexible and create strategies for success amid uncertainty. These are the lessons I want to teach you here. After all, I believe the best part of life is learning to change along the way.

I left the conference having learned some things about the industries, trends and expectations of the future; a belly full of pasta and lobster; and, moreover, I left with some clarity. I wanted to tell stories of navigating change and people's purpose emerging.

* * *

This book focuses on the themes of uncertainty, change, and emergence. From "what do you want to be when you grow up" in childhood to "what is your purpose in life" in adulthood, there is so much pressure to pick something specific to attain and then pursue it linearly.

Society, employers, and even loved ones often pressure us to prescribe our lives before we live them. What I want to share are the powerful stories of successful individuals who became successful *through* being adaptable in their purpose. I want to show that it's what one does *after* a decision or setting a course of action that is far more interesting, and a potential opportunity for growth, than merely making a plan and sticking to it. I want to empower others to be adaptable, too, as I have become more and more over the last two years, something I have found to be unnatural to me but very rewarding. Navigating what comes next is where the inevitable unexpected happens.

Things for which you can't plan. Things requiring a change in your vision or strategy.

Having worked with fifteen companies in five industries on strategy and company transformation, I have long enjoyed thinking about vision and strategy from the lens of a business. I fully believe that doing the hard work to understand the structure of an industry, the competitive dynamics, the trends that could shape the future, and the fundamental economics is critical. Developing a strategy by understanding who you are, the environment in which you play, and where and how you want to participate is the first step.

However, I learned a profound lesson after I advised a company undergoing a twenty-percent workforce reduction after an acquisition and shift in strategy toward a different area of the market. What you do after the strategy has been developed is just as important. While planning and preparing for the future can help position you for success, what is probably more influential in the outcome is the journey.

- How do you treat people and empower them along the way?
- How do you adapt to changing and dynamic conditions (like an unexpected CEO change and a delay in an IT system integration, in the case of the workforce reduction I worked on)?
- What are enablers for success and indicators of change?

These learnings shaped how I advise companies now: thinking through scenarios, risk mitigation tactics like rapid prototyping of new ideas, and ultimately preparing organizations to be more flexible and nimbler to change.

And on the personal side, since attending the University of Michigan's Ross School of Business and learning so much while in management consulting at Roland Berger, I personally utilize leadership frameworks and my own experimentation framework for personal development. These have led me to new hobbies, to losing forty-five pounds in the course of a year, and to explore more.

I wrote this book because I started noticing a pattern in conversations with friends, family, and colleagues. The theme was a feeling of discomfort in not knowing what they wanted to do in life (which often is thought to equate to who one wants to be or their life purpose). The more I thought about this, the more I heard it. At the same time, after identifying my topic during the conference in Boston, I read about, researched, and interviewed highly successful people who took a different outlook, embracing change and emergence in their lives. I think we all need to take the pressure "to become" off ourselves and rather embrace the ride.

My hope is, in reading this book, you will discover ideas for how to navigate uncertainty and to proactively and positively disrupt your life whenever you want to do so. In this book, I hope to instill the same sort of passion and excitement I have for experimenting my way through life in you. And then ultimately, I want you to see this book as a tool by providing a collection of frameworks and tactics to try at any time, by yourself or with a group to navigate life a little differently. We will explore these questions:

- What is the role of purpose and vision in my life?
- How can I navigate change that comes my way?
- How can I proactively and positively disrupt my life?

I will share stories and learnings from people in a variety of fields on how they have navigated life's inevitable unexpectedness. You'll learn about individuals and companies that have experienced change, tragedy, and opportunity, and how they chose to move forward. A couple examples from the book include:

- Katharine Graham—How Mrs. Graham navigated deep tragedy and insecurity to be recognized as a major influencer in American journalism and politics in the late 1900s.
- Michelle Obama—How Mrs. Obama navigated personal discovery and disruption to become a beloved First Lady of the United States who launched an important campaign to fight child obesity.

My hope is you will love this book if you have ever struggled with the question of what to do with your life, have tried to sit down and plan it out, and struggled. The audience of this book, then, is multifaceted: a person who is uncertain about what they want to do in life, someone feeling pressure about some major (or minor) decision in life, someone who wonders what else life might hold, or someone who simply is curious about frameworks that facilitate change, experimentation, and learning.

PART ONE

ALCHEMY

CHAPTER 1

WANDERING THE DESERT

―

One of the innate dilemmas of biography is that life is not much like a book. It rarely contains a clearly stated thesis, coherently developed. Life sprawls, stumbles, advances, retreats, gropes for the light switch, and once in a while makes intuitive leaps whose import is barely understood until later, if ever, by the leaper. Life seems to me an improvisation.

—JAN SWAFFORD

As we were packing up our laptops to head to the airport, the partner on my first management consulting project asks me, "Did you read *The Alchemist* yet?"

"Not yet," I replied shamefully, feeling like I probably should have by now since the project manager relayed the partner's request the week prior while I was in Germany for kick-off training.

"Read it. I first read this book by accident," he said. "I was boarding a plane and was about to put my luggage in the overhead bin when I saw it, just lying there in the overhead bin. It was probably left behind, so I grabbed it for plane reading and stored my luggage."

He continues, "Two hours later or so, the plane landed, I took my suitcase from the overhead bin, and put *The Alchemist* back in the overhead bin for someone else to read. Now, read it on your plane ride home, and you'll see why finding it in an overhead bin was meaningful to me. And why I want to share it with you, too."

I was a bit confused, wondering simultaneously, *Why would someone read a chemistry book in an overhead bin, and why is a chemistry book "meaningful" to him?*

But I just nodded and said, "Okay, yes, I'll read it on the plane ride home."

* * *

About a week prior to the partner of my first consulting project asking me if I had read *The Alchemist*, I had participated in my company's kick-off training in Germany for new consultants.

After graduating from the University of Michigan in May 2013 and having a couple months to move and vacation, I started working in management consulting in July. It was the second week of training in Germany (and essentially the third week of my career), and it was clear I was one of the most junior, experience-wise and age-wise, individuals in the group of fifty or so at this training. Most other countries in attendance required their consultants to have some tenure before sending them to this training.

Having attended Michigan Ross School of Business in undergrad, surrounded by many classmates who had parents or family members in business—while mine, now retired, were a teacher and an automobile factory assembly line worker—I was no stranger to being the "underdog" in business knowledge. Though our family dinner conversations had never included business, I wouldn't have traded them for the world—my parents loved me fiercely and taught me the value of hard work. And that's just what I would do here: work hard, work harder than the person next to me perhaps, and get up to speed bootstrap-style.

It was in the second week of training that I rushed back to my hotel room after a training session to read an email. I had been staffed on a project! My first consulting project.

In the email, the project manager gave a brief overview about the client, described that the project was focused on growth strategy, and provided travel information so I could book my travel. He emphasized I should focus on enjoying training but to buy and start reading the book *The Alchemist*, a book that the partner on the project from Boston requested all team members of the project read. Then he signed off.

The Alchemist? I hadn't heard of it. But I assumed that, since the client was in the chemicals industry, it had something to do with chemistry. What had I gotten myself into? I hadn't taken a chemistry class since AP Chemistry in high school. I felt a little uneasy with doubt but quickly ordered the book and headed to dinner.

***

DOUBT AS AN ALLY

Doubt. Connotations of this word include weakness, lack of clarity, instability. But consider it again.

In *The Alchemist* by Paolo Coelho, Santiago, the story's protagonist, is a young shepherd boy whose life is put on an uncertain path after an encounter with a woman who tells Santiago to follow the message in his dreams and seek treasure at the Egyptian pyramids. He is robbed, has to work unexpectedly, and undergoes many threats. He experiences doubt, time after time, *wondering if he made the right decision for his life* in leaving his home, his vocation, and his comfortable, or at least routine, life.[1]

With little but a dream and no real plan but to literally wander the desert in order find the treasure, Santiago sets off to uncover his treasure, leading him through a journey of self-doubt and revelation. Santiago starts to explore his many instances of doubt through inquiry.[2] You see, *doubt does not have to have negative connotations if channeled.* Doubt prompts us to think, to question why we doubt, and can be a powerful tool to find clarity.

I have doubts nearly every day: *Will I be able to add value in my client engagements; will I fall back into unhealthy eating and fitness habits again after a couple years in consulting; will I be able to have both a career and be a mother someday; are my priorities in line with God's will?*

---

[1] Paulo Coelho, *The Alchemist*.
[2] Ibid.

One lesson from the book that stood out to me occurred after Santiago was robbed. There were many possible ways he could have reacted to the sense of self-doubt he experienced when nothing in his journey seemed to be going right. Eventually, he chose to realize a lesson: in life, there are people who take. But not everyone is a taker. What is important is not to let takers take too much, such that your horizons are dimmed and you stop dreaming. Rather, stay on the path forward and keep following your dream.

This is, of course, easier said than done. Having been lied to and cheated on in relationships, I resonated with Santiago when he was robbed. At first, he questioned everything, including himself. In my own life, when I was "robbed," I questioned whether it, in some way, was my own fault. I doubted myself. It took a long time to realize that although I am flawed, it was not my fault. I was not responsible for takers. The doubting made me realize this and ultimately work through it. While I don't have a singular dream like Santiago's treasure, his approach resonates with me and my own fears because he did not let external, uncontrollable factors dictate his ability to dream. So, I will dream of family traditions and of enlightening business meetings.

In *The Alchemist*, Santiago gained experience and perspective. He acknowledged doubt time after time when uncertainty crept into his journey. And eventually, Santiago uncovered the greatest revelation of all, the world's greatest lie: "that at a certain point in our lives, we lose control of what's happening to us, and our lives become controlled by fate."[3]

---

3   Ibid.

Santiago learned that while it is true that we cannot control everything, and unfortunate things will come our way, we have control over what we do next. We have control over how doubt manifests—as a tool for destruction, inspiration, or exploration. Santiago learned that we have control over the lies we tell ourselves, whether to believe them, and choosing whether to wander the desert in search of a dream and treasure.

* * *

THE POWER OF QUESTIONS

One way many people take initiative in directing their lives is by setting a vision or defining their purpose. In Steven Covey's best-selling classic *7 Habits of Highly Effective People*, he explains the habit, "Begin with the end in mind"—to begin each day, task, or project with a clear vision of your desired direction and destination, and then make things happen. To succeed with developing this habit, people are encouraged to develop a personal statement of what one wants to be and do.[4]

Rather than disagreeing with having the end in mind, I have learned over the years that there is an additional lens to look through. This lens is that of inquiry in the process of deciding or setting a direction. Starting my consulting career with *The Alchemist* was fitting, as our recommendations and insights are only as good as the questions we ask. Santiago doubts, asks questions, and moves forward, leading to a final pondering for Santiago and the audience: *What do I hope to gain from the treasure and why?*

---

4   Stephen R. Covey, "Habit 2: Begin with the End in Mind."

In a conversation with one of my former MBA classmates, I posed, "Rather than say, 'I want to be a managing director at a top-tier investment bank and work in the consumer space,' ask yourself, 'What do I hope to gain, and what impact do I hope to have, should I become a managing director at a top-tier investment bank in the consumer space, and why?'" Thinking about that conversation made me realize the importance of the question we ask ourselves and how we answer it. To me, the statement should be less about a one-dimensional attainment of a position or specific outcome and more about the impact one is able to have.

Asking good questions has the power to unlock more about our motivations and the drivers for what might provide a sense of fulfillment. It also provides a healthy relationship with doubt, uncertainty, and the unexpected when plans go awry, as our true drivers and motivations can manifest in more than one path, vocation or otherwise. For my classmate above, if he does not attain this role someday, rather than failing, he can think through other ways to gain what he wanted to gain from this role in the first place, because the end is no longer the role itself

* * *

DISCOVERY ALCHEMY

While a type-A personality and very organized, I sometimes find myself procrastinating on new things or things requiring my best mental effort. Perhaps that's why I had put off starting *The Alchemist* during that week between training and the partner's inquiry. After all, I thought the book was about chemistry, a subject I had not touched in five years, and had a lingering doubt I was in over my head.

In just one week, I was filled with doubt. With the book, with the job, with this whole traveling schedule. I had only ever flown twice before this job. And now I was going to fly every week to work in an industry I knew nothing about for a client of whom I had never heard.

Nowadays, people might call what I was feeling "imposter syndrome." But truly, I had no experiences like this to draw from in the past. I didn't know what I didn't know. I didn't even know how to find out. I now had pages and pages of reports and documents to sift through. And, as I switched off my Blackberry for takeoff to Detroit, I had this book to read.

* * *

"Welcome to Detroit. It is now safe to use your hand-held mobile devices."

I was right. I didn't know what I didn't know. And in this case, I had no idea what *The Alchemist* was about. But 163 pages later, I did, or at least was starting to, after reading it. *The Alchemist* is and is not about alchemy.

Alchemy was a medieval chemistry, based on the supposed transformation of matter, specifically metals into gold.[5] While an alchemist character does appear in *The Alchemist,* he is not the protagonist of the alchemy that occurs in the book. Rather, I would argue it is Santiago himself who is transformed as he learns about himself and about his priorities. Santiago's

---

5 "Alchemy."

dream is transformed from buried treasure at the Egyptian pyramids to treasure realized in his heart.

As I reflected on alchemy after the plane landed, I grabbed my luggage from the overhead bin and stood up a little straighter, a small grin creeping onto my lips as I walked up the jet bridge and into the McNamara Terminal in Detroit.

Maybe I could do this, I thought. *Germany, traveling to Pennsylvania for a few months, chemicals, growth strategy, being a businesswoman.* All new and uncharted territory for me, but I would learn from the team. I would see doubt as a prompt for asking good questions, embracing doubt as an alley and leveraging the power of question. And I would see what the path held for me as I began my own journey of wandering the desert, or skies in my case.

* * *

TAKEAWAYS

What many of the stories I will tell in subsequent chapters teach is the importance of seeing our stories as unwritten, at least from the present perspective. Even for those individuals who seem to have "made it," there was doubt and questioning along the way. These were probably two allies in getting to where they did. And they may still be present companions.

In this way, seeing life as unwritten is an invitation to open our eyes to the possibilities that might emerge, the lessons that might come, and the growth expectantly around the corner (or waiting for us as we wander in our own version of the desert). Instead of prescribing or writing our lives before we live them, why not adopt a mindset of writing our lives each day as we live them, driving accountability and our ability to shape our lives down to the choice-by-choice level, which can still be within a broader vision or direction?

In one of my favorite films, *Dead Poets Society*, Professor Keating, an unusual teacher who challenged his students to seize the day and think for themselves, reads the boys a poem by Walt Whitman:

> **"Oh Me! Oh life!"** - By Walt Whitman
> *Oh me! Oh life! of the questions of these recurring,*
> *Of the endless trains of the faithless, of cities fill'd*
>   *with the foolish,*
> *Of myself forever reproaching myself, (for who*
>   *more foolish than I, and who more faithless?)*
> *Of eyes that vainly crave the light, of the objects*
>   *mean, of the struggle ever renew'd,*
> *Of the poor results of all, of the plodding and sordid crowds I see around me,*
> *Of the empty and useless years of the rest, with the*
>   *rest me intertwined,*
> *The question, O me! so sad, recurring—What good*
>   *amid these, O me, O life?*
> *Answer.*
> *That you are here—that life exists and identity,*
> *That the powerful play goes on, and you may contribute a verse*[6]

---

6 Walt Whitman, "Oh Me! Oh Life!"

In the Introduction to this book, I revealed that it took me some time in deciding what to write about—*what could I write a book about?* And for me that became the beauty of this book—the evolution, the research, the stories, the reflection. And then the writing. I became fascinated with learning how people's lives emerge, and how uncertainty is navigated. I heard many MBA classmates wonder if they had taken full advantage of the MBA experience, and whether their ending point was worth it or the "right" path.

And we've all heard similar things that cause people to question their life path—where do you see yourself in five years? What do you want your next promotion to be? What is your purpose in life? What is your legacy? These questions are good, and they almost certainly cause doubt and elicit inquiry, as they pose: what will you write your life about?

What I have learned is you write it every day by the choices you make. And tomorrow, you have another opportunity to pick up the pen and write some more. I think there is much power in taking the weight of prescribing our lives off our shoulders. How do you succeed after all in a world that wants us to prescribe so much—when so much of what we know will change tomorrow?

Our life is emergent. Our life is unwritten. Our life stumbles forward sometimes. In American composer and author Jan Swafford's book, *Charles Ives: A Life of Music,* he writes, "life sprawls, stumbles, advances, retreats, gropes for the light switch, and once in a while makes intuitive leaps whose import is barely understood until later, if ever, by the leaper. Life seems to me an improvisation."[7]

---

[7] Jan Swafford, *Charles Ives: A Life with Music.*

LOOKING AHEAD

And so, to Mr. Keating, Walt Whitman, and Jan Swafford, I'd say: nevertheless, let us emerge. Let us take up the pen and write. Let us stumble. For, like the beauty of creativity is that it can fail, the beauty in life is living it—emerging from the planned and the unplanned, having a laugh and a cry along the way.

In Dead Poets Society, Professor Keating orally verbalizes Walt Whitman's poem to his students and follows with: "What will your verse be?"[8]

What I invite readers in this book to do is first, to consider the popular practice of setting a vision or writing a purpose statement; second, to listen and learn about the stories and lives of people who have navigated uncertainty, sometimes tragedy; and third, to consider some frameworks, practices, and actions that anyone, with a team or as an individual, can adopt any time to navigate an uncertain, un-prescribed but rich-with-possibility life.

We will explore stories of people who have wrestled with change and wandered their version of the desert, like Santiago. And I will ask questions, like Santiago, in recounting these stories of people who have navigated uncertainty. Specifically, think about the following:

- How do expert "navigators of life" think? How do successful, "emergent" lives come about?
- How do you grow your potential and capabilities in all directions?

---

8   Walt Whitman, "Oh Me! Oh Life!"

- What questions should you be asking yourself, and when? How do you know when to swerve or pivot?
- Whom do you surround yourself with along the way?
- How can you stay emergent and curious when "life happens?"
- And one last consideration: a key theme I want readers to take away from this chapter and from this book is not to believe the lies we tell ourselves. Remembering Santiago from *The Alchemist*, we will doubt, and we may even tell ourselves we cannot do something, be someone, go somewhere. Santiago experienced doubt time and time again wandering the desert, as I did time and time again wandering the skies during my consulting travels, wondering if "imposter syndrome" would ever go away, and if I had finally reached the limit for what I could do.

But in doing so, by seeing doubt as a reason to limit ourselves and turn back, we are also prescribing our lives by limiting them. We are telling ourselves lies. I invite you instead to consider:

- What are these lies for you?
- How might you see doubt differently, not as a reason to limit but as a reason to inquire and explore?
- The next time you're wandering a desert and experience doubt, be aware of it. Make it your alley. And ask yourself, what verse will you write this time?

In my experience, good questions and even better insights will arise.

CHAPTER 2

VISION AND PURPOSE

Every time you are tempted to react in the same old way, ask if you want to be a prisoner of the past or a pioneer of the future.

Walk with those seeking truth. . . . Run from those who think they've found it.

—DEEPAK CHOPRA

"Do you ever think about what you want your leadership style to be?" I asked my boyfriend Leon as he gripped the steering wheel and took us around another turn. We were driving the Great Ocean Road between the Victorian cities of Torquay and Allansford near Melbourne, Australia.

"I've thought about the leaders that I admire and want to be like. I had a manager who was always able to think at a more strategic level than those around her. But I guess I've never articulated what I want my leadership style to be," he replied.

"What about your purpose?" I inquired. "The next cycle in our mentorship program is about purpose."

"Yes, all the time. Especially lately, since signing my offer for post-grad school." He continued, "I can't help but wonder how long I'm going to be in banking and what's the next step."

"I know what you mean. While at Booth, we've explored so many different options, from startups to launching our own business and more, especially for you, with your private equity and venture capital internships." I paused. "But, I mean, what if that's not enough? Are we impacting people's lives? Are we fulfilling our purpose?"

"I guess we need to think about what that purpose is first. In the meantime, I'm pulling over. Look at this view!" And with that, he pulled into the scenic turnout parking area, we grabbed our phones, and took some of the most beautiful pictures of horizon over the seemingly limitless ocean. I couldn't help but think that its majesty and limitlessness echoed the possibilities for our lives, should we choose to take them.

HOW DO WE CRAFT A VISION OR PURPOSE STATEMENT?

In January of 2019, as a part of a Christian leaders in business mentorship program in Chicago, my group started a module on purpose. By the end of the cycle, we were supposed to have a drafted a personal purpose statement. Over the course of a month, my group had various discussions and conducted several activities with our mentor to think about the "special work" God has laid out for everyone. This could be a specific vocation or career or could go further.

The module on purpose suggested that purpose is more akin to one's calling. It is the reason for being, or "a mission of service," found at the intersection of one's SHAPE (strengths, heart, areas of interest, personality, and experiences) and a need in the world. Thus, there is internal and external reflection. Each need in the world possesses both a "what" and a "who." The program, as well as other guides on purpose and vision writing, acknowledge that since our SHAPE develops over time, the expression of our purpose or vision for our lives in a statement is an iterative process that unfolds over time as well.[9]

This part of the mentorship program was more challenging for me than others. Even though I had utilized many tools to understand and reflect on my strengths (e.g. strengths finder), personality (e.g. Myers-Briggs, social styles, and more), and so on, I felt limited by the purpose statement I had constructed through this module. Perhaps I didn't get it quite right, or perhaps I was feeling that writing the statement was forced.

In retrospect, I think I was just placing too much pressure on myself to distill the right words rather than view the exercise as a reflection of my SHAPE and how it can be used in my life. It continues to be an exercise I reflect upon, which is likely its intent all along. For now, my draft statement focuses on glorifying God by using my strengths in ideation and pragmatism to bring structure and action to abstract thought, helping people and companies change for the better.

I learned through this process the importance of writing a statement that does not have a finite end. In the previous

---

[9] Kevin Leman and William Pentak, *The Way of the Shepherd: 7 Ancient Secrets to Managing Productive People.*

chapter, I referenced a conversation with a fellow MBA classmate, questioning whether his career path was going to be fulfilling when he articulated it as attaining the top title in the organization. We both learned that, rather than the end being about a one-dimensional attainment of a position or specific outcome, a fulfilling end is more about the impact one can have. In this way, the job is never done, perhaps because the impact can be spread further or perhaps because it evolves into something new.

Many believe that simply getting something on paper or typed out can be useful. Common prompts for writing include:

- "The special work that I am set apart for is . . ."
- "The purpose of my unique design is . . ."
- "My purpose is . . ."
- "My superpower is . . . and I want to use it to . . ."

Common questions to think about include:

- "Who do I want to be?"
- "What do I want to accomplish?"
- "How can I use my strengths, heart, areas of interest, personality, and experiences?"
- "What would I want someone to say I worked toward at my funeral?"

The statement is meant to focus on who you want to be, what you want to do, or what you want to be known for, reaffirming who you are and putting your goals in focus. Various frameworks and tools are available to help us reflect on ourselves to inform our purpose. This book, however, is about what you do after this first step of reflecting on vision and purpose, since I believe what follows is just as important as writing a vision or purpose statement in the first place. My brief discussion above about how to craft a vision or purpose statement should serve only as an initial reference for reflection, but I encourage readers to explore the topics more.

WHEN DO WE CRAFT A VISION OR PURPOSE STATEMENT?

More and more young people are pushed to take an internship earlier and earlier, such that rising juniors in an undergraduate program already have two to three roles under their belt. Through these experiences, students start to explore and understand what opportunities are available to them. They start to learn about how their interests match up against these opportunities. The question of what role for what end is considered earlier and earlier. My belief is that students should be wary of narrowing too early before they are able to fully explore and discover where their interests may lie.

Many scholars, from professors to assistant deans at premier schools, suggest the importance for students in high school, college, and university to gain exposure to potential professional or vocational experiences, to explore skillsets and network, or even task-oriented jobs that help teach time management. In addition, working part-time helps fund schooling and provides lessons in responsibility and accountability. Experiences inside and outside of the classroom can be leveraged to intentionally decide who they are, who they want to be, and what career choice best suits their vision or purpose.[10]

In my undergraduate years, I did take a number of roles, from a student custodian for the summer camps coming through the dorms at the University of Michigan, to a research assistant, to an administrative assistant at a driving school, to a resident advisor, to eventually a financial planning analysis intern at a five-billion-dollar corporation. While I ended up having several interesting roles, many of my peers had two or three very impressive internship experiences by the summer before senior year; this is even more true for students today.

I was fortunate enough to land a role in the management consulting industry, but recruiting has only gotten more competitive over time. According to *Harvard Business Review*, recent graduates are more likely to be underemployed, i.e. in jobs that don't require a college degree, today than between 1998 and 2003. Additionally, earnings inequality among recent graduates has increased, so the bottom quarter of recent graduates make less today than they have in the past.[11]

Students need to think about who they are, what they want, and what set of experiences they might need to assemble to be attractive for a role they think they want. The merit of whether middle-schoolers and high-schoolers should be thinking very seriously about internships and careers, and the bridge between the two, can be debated. I would argue

---

10 Stephanie K. Eberle, "A Marathon, Not a Sprint."
11 Jed Kolko, "What the Job Market Looks Like for Today's College Graduates."

there likely are some downsides of prescribing a path too early, but the fact is people are being prompted in many ways to confront vision and purpose earlier and earlier.

So when is the right time to go through the discovery process to craft a vision for our lives or purpose statement? Commonly "appropriate" times in our lives to undergo such a discovery process is a "life change." A life change might be from a professional perspective, such as considering a career change, whether to pursue a promotion, or whether to quit your job and pursue an MBA degree. Or a life change might be from a personal perspective, such as when considering getting married, getting divorced, after a loved one's death, or upon a spiritual or religious conversion.

Regardless of whether there is something prompting the questions, I believe, as the title of this book suggests, that we are made to change. Therefore, any time is the right time to positively disrupt your life. Our time to learn about ourselves does not end when we choose a first career path. Our time to learn about ourselves does not end when we make a personal life choice about where to live or whom to spend our lives with. In my view, a vision or purpose statement can be explored anytime and may prompt change and disruption, which can be embraced as a positive part of growing and learning.

WHY WE CRAFT A VISION OR PURPOSE STATEMENT
The underlying drivers behind why people write purpose statements or vision statements are very much like a company's reasons. We feel the need to maximize the value of our lives in a similar way that shareholders wish for shareholder value to be maximized. Purpose and vision provide direction. They can act

as a guiding compass against which to think through personal and professional life decisions so we do not veer off course.

The statement creates priorities and produces a plan of action, or at least implies forthcoming action. It inspires deliberation on what to focus on. And in some ways, having a sense of direction just makes us feel good.

As a management consultant, I have worked with many corporations on setting a vision and strategy. In many cases, the results are presented to a board of directors and the impacts result in strategic decisions like acquisitions. Thus, the work can be very useful to set direction and priorities and even gain approval for financial capital deployment.

In a client engagement, we begin by seeking to understand the current situation; then determining the complications both externally, in the market, and internally, in the organization—then distilling the compelling question(s) at hand. Our work then determines resolution options and a path forward. As a part of this process, sound strategic thinking identifies indicators that would suggest positive evidence for a pivot among options, or even a reevaluation altogether. Since we seek truth as professional advisors, we acknowledge it can be in the best interest of a company to change course, extend the questions being asked, and/or give news the client may not want to hear.

This approach in business is not unlike the process of reflecting on one's purpose. In business, sticking to a direction or vision for too long without acknowledging indicators for change might lead to becoming obsolete in a fast-changing industry shaped by technology and under the influence of new entrants. I believe it is also true that sound reflection should seek to identify indicators for disruption and change. Our potential as humans is incredibly dynamic and is influenced by experiences. Therefore, the need to maximize the value of our lives might actually be resolved through change.

CONSIDERATIONS TO EXPLORE

What I have learned is it can be useful to self-reflect and write a draft statement to guide your direction. I would recommend considering the following:

- What are your key strengths, heart characteristics, areas of interest, personality traits, and experiences?
- How do these add to your unique design, or superpower?
- How do you want to use these in your life?

Try drafting a purpose statement, like "I want to use my _____ to create/help/impact _____." Then I would encourage you to invest time thinking about what to do next, because I have found what comes next is just as interesting and important to explore:

- How might I break down my purpose into nearer-term goals to accomplish? What are some experiments I can conduct to reach these goals?
- What are some hobbies, activities, or networks I can develop to grow toward my purpose? What skills or capabilities would help me have greater impact?
- Who can I talk to, whether for an informational interview, coaching, or mentorship, who might have an interesting perspective or skillset related to my interests?

By taking a step or two rather than trying to accomplish one's purpose statement all at once, you start the journey of making the statement real. You also open yourself up to learning more about your interests, noticing the indicators, and realizing when a pivot is the next step. In the next chapter, I recount a few stories where noticing indicators and working through how they impact the vision is critical for survival.

PART TWO

STORIES OF CHANGE

CHAPTER 3

WHEN VISION GOES WRONG

Even when you think you have your life all mapped out; things happen that shape your destiny in ways you might never have imagined.

—DEEPAK CHOPRA

"I can't believe that I'm even thinking about running again right now," I said, still full-body panting as Leon and I made our way back to the hotel shuttle after running a marathon. "But I am just so excited that now I can do five-mile runs a few times a week, or breeze through a quick three-mile run to stay fit when I start work again." I day-dreamed about how much time I would save being able to get in quick runs, setting a vision for how I wanted my exercise routine to evolve.

"That's great, and I agree. There are two things that I want to make sure I keep up after going back to work: church on Sunday mornings and running a few times a week," Leon concurred.

"It just means so much to me. There was a point during the marathon when I saw scenes from my life flash before my eyes, from running the mile as a fifth grader and throwing up after to feeling bad about not being able to keep up on a hike in Colorado," I recounted. "I couldn't help but tear up thinking about how much this means to me and how it is changing my life for the better."

The next week and a half, Leon and I celebrated the winter quarter and the marathon by going with a group of graduate school students to the Philippines for spring break. When we got back, I met up with a few friends for Taco Tuesday to catch up from the last few weeks.

"Hey guys, my Uber is here, so I'm going to head out. It was so great to see you," and turning I pushed the door with one arm, purse balancing in that hand, looking down at my phone in the other hand to see what the license plate of the Uber was. *Gosh, this street is not well-lit*, I thought.

"Ahh," I yelled as I suddenly found myself falling. *Crunch.* And immediately I knew something wasn't right. I had missed the fact that there was a big drop between the restaurant's floor and the street level. I started to stand and couldn't put weight on my ankle.

That night I came to terms with the fact I was going to be on crutches for a couple days, and my ankle was badly sprained. What I didn't know that night was I wouldn't be able to run again for seven weeks. My training and progress from the marathon weren't going to see me run five miles a few times a week just like that. I would have to start again, on a return-to-run program after physical therapy. It is a life lesson I'll never forget.

* * *

While setting a vision or purpose can provide direction and guidelines against which to think through decisions, doing so can be met with challenges. If your first steps try to go too big too quickly, for example, you might have, as the colloquialism says, "put the cart before the horse," leading to potentially disastrous decisions requiring significant resources to fix.

You might also set an incredibly lofty vision, and the worst could happen, completely beyond your control, leading to degradation of the team, self-deprecation, and a sense of being lost if not able to rally the team. Or, in order to get you steps closer to your vision, you make decisions or take actions that have unknown but detrimental consequences that shift the path completely.

Many things can happen to lead one astray, question one's vision, and affect others along the way. I want to provide a few examples of when setting a vision or purpose can go wrong to highlight the importance of keeping your eyes and heart open to change after the vision is defined.

THE CASE OF THE TRANS-ANTARCTIC EXPEDITION: WHEN VISION LEADS YOU TO THE EDGE
In *Leading at the Edge: Leadership Lessons from the Extraordinary Saga of Shackleton's Antarctic Expedition*, Dennis Perkins primarily focuses on the realization that being "led to the edge," meaning experiencing extreme challenges or the ultimate crucible of human endeavors in

the pursuit of a vision, reveals the essence of leadership. The book recounts and analyzes Ernest Shackleton's expedition to traverse Antarctica.[12] Around the same time, another explorer named Stefansson was also trying to cross Antarctica.[13] Both men had a vision to accomplish a never-before-accomplished feat, and set about attaining their visions in the early 1900s.

Shackleton recruited a team of men and was said to have displayed the famous ad, "Men wanted for hazardous journey, small wages, bitter cold, long months of complete darkness, constant danger, safe return doubtful, honor and recognition in case of success." While there are some who believe the ad to be a myth and the visionary character of Shackleton to be exaggerated, the book by Perkins suggests a number of leadership lessons that can applied to lives in the present.[14]

Shackleton is recounted to have led his crew to safety while the crew led by Stefansson, the other explorer attempting the same feat, disintegrated into a group of self-interested individuals where ultimately many died.[15] Perkins suggests that Shackleton's relative success in almost certain peril shows the importance of the following principles:

---

[12] Dennis Perkins, Margaret Holtman, and Jillian B. Murphy, *Leading at the Edge: Leadership Lessons from the Extraordinary Saga of Shackleton's Antarctic Expedition.*

[13] "Never Give Up, Don't Be Afraid to Lead."

[14] Joshua Horn, "Shackleton's Ad — Men Wanted for Hazardous Journey."

[15] "Never Give Up, Don't Be Afraid to Lead."

1. Never lose sight of the ultimate goal, and focus energy on short-term objectives.
2. Set a personal example with visible, memorable symbols and behaviors.
3. Instill optimism and self-confidence but stay grounded in reality.
4. Take care of yourself: Maintain your stamina and let go of guilt.
5. Reinforce the team message constantly: "We are one—we live or die together."
6. Minimize status differences and insist on courtesy and mutual respect.
7. Master conflict—deal with anger in small doses, engage dissidents, and avoid needless power struggles.
8. Find something to celebrate and something to laugh about.
9. Be willing to take the Big Risk.
10. Never give up—there's always another move.[16]

While Shackleton and his rival Stefansson each had a similar vision, their outcomes are more interesting to ponder. Both men's visions failed. But Shackleton's crew came back alive while Stefansson's did not. The principles of leadership that Perkins identifies above are meant to identify why the outcome was different. Ultimately, Shackleton's vision itself had to be abandoned to survive.

The vision led Shackleton and his crew "to the edge" to begin with, which can be beneficial in certain situations to understand one's limits and ultimately be tested in the

---

16 "Learning at the Edge: Notes & Review."

most dramatic way. But it was Shackleton's willingness to adjust, not cling to the vision, and drive toward new, short-term goals that require concrete, decisive action that allowed to team to survive. The act of doing something, even if small, creates momentum, and several small wins can be more fruitful, or in Shackleton's case necessary, than trying to tackle a grand feat in a vacuum. This comes through in Perkins' first lesson in leadership above: *"Never lose sight of the ultimate goal, and focus energy on short-term objectives."*[17]

The bookend of these lessons, number ten, is also interesting when thinking about vision and purpose: *"Never give up—there's always another move."* Creativity is celebrated by the authors as a means for innovating through tough circumstances. Perkins highlights in this lesson the importance of having a degree of expectation for things to go wrong, but that it is important to keep moving.

The ability to try something, "fail fast" as the agile approach says, try something else, and so on is almost more important in dynamic and changing circumstances, which is very much like our everyday lives. Critical thinking, effort, and not bowing out on commitments is important, but the ability to "never give up" and "make another move" takes pressure off getting everything "right" on the path toward the vision and institutes momentum.

---

17   Ibid.

THE CASE OF SUREPAYROLL®: A VISION IN JEOPARDY

SurePayroll is now a leading small business payroll company providing easy online payroll services. While now owned by Paychex® Company, SurePayroll was once a fledgling startup with the vision of helping small businesses outsource payroll.[18]

SurePayroll's selling point was in being the first online provider that also understood payroll laws. The problem they solve is two-fold: reducing the need for small businesses to put time, focus, and resources into payroll and reducing the risk of inaccurate or late payroll filing, which incurs IRS fines. SurePayroll differentiated itself at the time from other payroll services by its use of the internet and electronic processing, facilitating more affordable rates for small businesses.[19]

The challenge experienced at SurePayroll in reaching its vision to grow and be a successful company providing online payroll services was driven by several factors, an important one of which was having a lofty vision and missing important steps in the journey when the allure of the big break arose. SurePayroll had the opportunity to enter a strategic partnership with a large bank in the United States. While the company's decision to pursue the partnership led to eventual success, the vision was put in jeopardy along the way. From not having consistent and standard operational processes in place that had been proven to work for customers to having product issues upon engaging a strategic partner, the startup experienced incredible pressure and demands early on.[20]

---

18   "Paychex Completes Acquisition of SurePayroll."
19   "About Us: We Can Help With Your Small Business Payroll Needs."
20   Michael Alter, "Embracing Your Fear," (session three).

Due to its state of selling while building, which in the startup world is a necessity to stay afloat, SurePayroll likely employed the "Wizard of Oz" approach through flintstoning—that is, what appeared to customers to be automated was actually people manually carrying out tasks on the backend.[21] Startups thus evolve operations through knowing and possibly mapping out the various processes, activities, and tasks needed for an online payroll system. However, it presented risks because this approach cannot sustain a significant increase in customers before being automated, as intended for the business model.

SurePayroll experienced its first huge operational challenge after going live with a big customer. The orders coming in from the partnership crashed SurePayroll's systems, and onboarding was chaotic. It would be easy to say the timing of the bank partnership was too early, but in the startup world, you may only have one chance at such a customer. Often, processes are not yet documented, but the eventual success of the business could be propelled by a large customer. At the same time, it is important to be prepared to keep up. On the individual level, it is one thing to set a vision, but it is an entirely different thing to put in the work and create the short-term objectives to build the processes or endurance to get there. It takes incredible discipline, again akin to Gladwell's *Outliers*.

Furthermore, in a startup where time is quite literally money, leadership can leave managing people as a secondary priority. Leadership might swing so far to process management that management falters. In the Antarctica expedition example

---

21   Amy Hoy, "The Fine Art of 'Flinstoning.'"

previously described, understanding people was a key driver for why one expedition brought all its people back and one did not. Similarly, in our pursuits of vision and purpose, it is important not to lose sight of the trees within the forest, otherwise success might be quite lonely.

Besides, people in our lives are dynamic and can be positively disruptive, spurring creativity and innovation. Slowing down enough to be aware of people can lead to important realizations about vulnerabilities or ideas for the vision or for a better one.

In the case of SurePayroll, the ultimate vision was not necessarily in question or unclear, but the path to get there was challenging, fraught with mishaps that through better structured short-term objectives might have been more manageable. Aligning priorities, setting up a project management office, and utilizing tools can facilitate movement. In the same way, how we go about our journeys—whether through an experimentation approach, leadership framework that works for you, or otherwise—can be more important than the specified end.

As mentioned, SurePayroll had a very successful sale to Paychex, so things worked out well for the company and leadership. But there were important lessons pertaining to setting a vision and when a vision is in jeopardy: don't forget the steps required to take the journey. While SurePayroll was a startup, and not an individual person, there is a translatable lesson in that going from vision to traction to scale is incredibly challenging. As *Outliers: The Story of Success* by Malcolm Gladwell suggests, it is often effort, energy, and perseverance that make the difference in being a successful outlier.[22]

THE CASE OF BLUE STRIPES CACAO SHOP: WHEN VISION STALLS BUT CHOCOLATE RISES

If you've ever strolled through New York City's East Village since June 2018 and not stopped at Blue Stripes Cacao Shop, go and do it. Take in everything inside, from the bookcase in the back, to the quotes on every mug and plate, to the messages in the decor, to the incredible aromas of cacao and succulent chocolate treats, to the smiling baristas brewing up the next delectable cup. Then, look up the story of how this gem on 13th Street came to be. It all started with a vision to be a writer.

Over a couple of decades ago, after taking a government-subsidized pastry course upon completion of military service in Israel, Oded Brenner, an aspiring writer, went on a chocolate journey in Paris with master chocolatier, Michele Chaudun, the owner of a chocolate store with the vibe Oded sought as inspiration for his true dream of writing.

Throughout the journey and beyond, Mr. Brenner chased inspiration and materials in pursuit of his writing career, as he strongly desired to make his writing vision happen. Along the journey, Oded created the Max Brenner chocolate brand, opened chocolate restaurants around the world, invented some chocolate treats, all while not writing much at all.

---

22   Malcolm Gladwell, *Outliers: The Story of Success.*

Even more unexpectedly, as the vision of being an esteemed writer stalled, a New York judge issued a "stipulated order" mandating that Oded could not say, make, or tell anyone anything about chocolate. This was a result of a legal battle with Israeli food and beverage company Strauss that had bought the Max Brenner chain form Oded Brenner in 2001. They took issue with Oded opening a coffee shop in New York, citing breach of contract, placing restrictions on chocolate in the coffee shop, eventually leading to its demise.

After an eleven-year legal battle, Oded signed a non-compete agreement and was exiled from the chocolate world for five years, having lost equity in Max Brenner, money, and hope in a new vision after the stall and an old one.

While this again stalled what might have been the beginning of a new vision, Oded himself did not stall, but rather started telling stories to his daughter about chocolaty adventures from his past and those that might one day be using chocolate as his pen and paper, his mediums to write.

In 2017, he traveled to the Blue Mountains in Jamaica and learned about cacao, the fruit from which chocolate is made. After a series of revelations about cacao and how it can be used, such as creating treats with its pulp and its beans, Oded was inspired to share his revelations with everyone when his chocolate exile ended, through a chocolate and coffee shop, Blue Stripes Cacao Shop in East Village. Oded embraced the connection he felt to the cacao's wildness to launch a new idea in experimenting with chocolate, exploring the fruit's full culinary value.

Oded himself says, "Life happens while you're planning other things, and that's what happened to me."[23]

Oded Brenner went from obliged military man to aspiring writer to chocolate student with a dream to still be a writer to a brand founder to a chocolate-everything exile to an explorer of and experimenter with cacao. In this adventure of a chocolate shop after release from exile, Brenner tells his story through short pieces of text written to his daughter throughout the shop. He says of cacao, "It never gets old or tiring."[24]

The way in which Oded feels about cacao, that it has depth and more to experiment with, mirrors how his life played out—he traversed from one failed vision to the next. I have a feeling his story will continue to be one of wild experimentation, revealing nuggets, or nibs in the language of cacao, of beauty, like the pulp and beans of cacao.

* * *

From this story, as well as those of Shackleton and SurePayroll, I learned to just keep moving, exploring, and experimenting with what might be possible. When I learned I had a badly sprained ankle, I was devastated. My vision for easy runs and simple fitness were put on hold. And because I knew my body and history with running in the past, I knew I would lose most of the progress I had made and would have to start over.

---

23 Michelle Divon, "Barred from Chocolate for 5 Years, Max Brenner Founder Makes a Sweet Comeback."

24 Ibid.

But that's just what I did. I started physical therapy and eventually began a return-to-run program. My vision was different now—I just wanted to get back to being able to do something I loved and that made me feel free. I learned that sometimes life will interrupt our journeys, changing our paths.

I would encourage anyone in such a situation to think about what orthodoxy would say is a reasonable reaction. List them out, then flip them on their heads. I did this after the ankle sprain and started experimenting with other activities. I started taking boxing classes, spin classes, and various yoga classes. While I like them all, I particularly like boxing, my own personal cacao nib, which I might have never discovered had my vision not been interrupted. Plus, I'm running again, thanks to solid physical therapy.

Blue Stripes Cacao Store in East Village, like Michele Chaudun's chocolate store in Paris for Oded Brenner, became an oasis for me in the writing of this book. I learned to unashamedly take a break and enjoy the aromas and the story around me. Perhaps one thought or story needed to be abandoned, or the vision for a point needed to be altered. While establishing a vision or purpose can be helpful, it is what happens when the vision goes wrong that is truly interesting. How do we react? How do we treat people while being pushed to the edge? Do we decide to give up on our dream or stay open to new discoveries? To me, it is at the edge of giving up on vision or figuring out a different path where our lives are built and emerge.

CHAPTER 4

WHEN LACK OF VISION GOES RIGHT

―

As we forge ahead, while we imagine what might be, we must rely on our guiding principles, our intentions, and our goals—not on being able to see and react to what's coming before it happens.

—ED CATMULL

EMERGE FROM THE DEEP: HOW HIKING THE GRAND CANYON REQUIRES BEING COMFORTABLE VISIONLESS
At 6:50 a.m. one May morning, I boarded a bus with my partner, Leon, to the South Kabab trailhead of the Grand Canyon.

A few minutes into the bus ride, the driver says, "So, how far is everyone going today?"

"To the river (the bottom) and back," we said. The driver quickly stated, "That's not recommended."

We got off the bus and went to fill our water bags—asking for help as we had never filled a three-gallon water bag. A park ranger asked how far we were going. Again, we were told "that's not recommended." Yet, we started down the trailhead, unprepared save our three-gallon water bags, some beef jerky, peanuts, and sour gummy worms.

Around 11:30 am, we reached the river, sore in the knees from the hike down. We both collapsed onto the soft grass by the river and proceeded to peel off our hiking boots and socks. The Arizona heat was building, so we stayed in the shade of the trees by the river. I reached in our pack for the jerky and peanuts and we feasted, for all that it was. An hour later, it was already time to head up the eleven-mile Bright Angel trail. We redressed and set on our way.

The first couple of miles were comparatively easy, as we weren't gaining much elevation. Leon and I were still getting to know each other, as it had only been a couple months since we'd met. We talked politics, societal issues, religion, and about our families. Leon was in better shape than I was. He has a naturally athletic form, where he maintains a six-pack and the ability to run a few miles without much maintenance. But I was keeping up, at least for now.

The miles and hours passed and with each hour, I noted that it didn't seem we had ascended much (hence why the hiking was comparatively easy). We were still so deep inside the canyon that I had lost sight of the vastness of the outside world and couldn't make out the path we would follow. We had no vision or knowledge of what lay ahead. With no other option and with the lingering doubt we had made a wrong turn, our strategy was existential, to *just keep moving*.

With the cliffs surrounding, I asked a park ranger at a water stop how we would crest the cliff and she pointed (though I couldn't entirely see toward what) to a series of switch-backs. With the park ranger's experienced guidance, we continued.

It soon became clear that I could never have done this alone. Leon, my hiking partner, fellow University of Chicago Booth MBA student, and now boyfriend, was there. In those last two miles, he told me we were almost at the top and we could do it. Resisting the temptation of distraction and being overwhelmed by the distance, we focused on the task at hand, setting small goals to put a switch-back behind us.

In the last quarter mile, I had straggled, and he came back for me, grabbed my hand, and we emerged together, a team. And we were different, would always be different. We had accomplished something together, something we booked two weeks before with no training or expertise in real hiking. And we had survived.

* * *

Reflecting on the most challenging hike of my life to date, I find that the journey was filled with lessons. While I would not suggest that someone attempt to hike the Grand Canyon unprepared, I do think that it is inevitable for us to be in situations that require the ability to act with no vision.

While expertise and preparedness are important, commitment, focus, and satisfying near-term needs (such as food and water in the case of the hike) are crucial to overcoming what seems impossible. While sometimes people advise against the impossible, remember what Henry Ford said: "Whether you think you can or think you can't, you're right." I say, take on big ideas and experiments—just remember stay nourished, body, mind, or soul, so you are not pouring from an empty cup.

A second theme emerged during the hike, that many small steps add up over time to significant mileage. If you just keep staring at the top of the cliff, you'll never feel any closer; it's the small steps and putting one switchback after another behind you that gets you somewhere. In these moments, use a strategy of "just keep moving" when it seems there is no other option.

Finally, in a third theme, I learned to not go it alone—ask for guidance and advice from a trusted expert, like the mountain ranger in the canyon. Lean on your teammates and encourage them, as well, like Leon and I did for each other. Such experiences build deep connections with others that create a culture of resiliency and understanding beyond what facts and figures can teach. Seek and be willing and courageous enough to give feedback, to help ensure that each step and each switchback is worthwhile.

THE ANTI-VISION: HOW LOU GERSTNER TURNED IBM AROUND, SAYING "WE DON'T NEED A VISION."

In *Who Says Elephants Can't Dance?*, Lou Gerstner describes one of the most impressive and important turnarounds of a major corporation in our nation's history. Gerstner was brought in as CEO of IBM in 1993 essentially to save the company. Perhaps what no one truly expected was not only did he help save IBM, but he also turned it around and facilitated its transformation.[25]

One of the most unexpected parts of this turnaround story is the doubt Gerstner experienced early on when he realized his lack of technical competency in a business where everything was, by its very nature, technical or about technology. But by thinking about why people believed in him despite his technical experience, he realized he needed to lead and have the courage to go against the grain—e.g. by keeping the pieces of IBM together rather than separating the pieces of the business.

Upon entering IBM as CEO, he had few preconceived notions about what was in the belly of the beast, so he did not have his own thesis on the path forward. Many of the early days and months were spent purely understanding the business and, most importantly, the people dynamics in the business—how people worked together, how decisions were made, and what symptoms might point to deeply-rooted issues that had to be rooted out.

In a communication to all IBM employees all over the world, Lou Gerstner says,

"Clearly, what we have been doing isn't working. We lost $16 billion in three years. Since 1985, more than 175,000 employees have lost their jobs. The media and our competitors are calling us a dinosaur. Our customers are unhappy and angry. We

---

25 Louis V. Gerstner, Jr., *Who Says Elephants Can't Dance?*

are not growing like our competitors. Don't you agree that something is wrong and that we should try something else?"[26]

This talk acknowledged that there was something wrong with the vision IBM once set for itself and that the company had to reevaluate or would likely go under.

What people didn't expect, especially Wall Street, was that Lou Gerstner also said, "We don't need a vision"[27]—there was more to it, of course, but this is what the media was in uproar about. People jumped on his words, questioning his ability to lead IBM out of irrelevancy.

But as we know, IBM is still around and even more relevant through Gerstner's tenure (he retired in 2002). IBM was in a new heyday. Gerstner is viewed as a legend; he emphasized early on that IBM didn't need a strategy or a vision but rather pointed to taking actions to address key issues within the business: "we don't need a 'vision' right now . . . we just need to keep moving."[28] The second part of Gerstner's quote went mostly unacknowledged by the media.

Again, we see the importance of taking small steps to move forward. Gerstner eventually cast a vision once he had a clear understanding of the market, the customers, and the foundational knowledge and capabilities within the business. But he did not cast one superficially. At the same time, he did not stall movement. He observed, he learned, he engaged

---

26 Ibid.

27 Ibid.

28 Ibid.

people, he began slow movement, eventually deciding on the direction.

One of the themes I am repeating is the importance of not getting too bogged down by the prospect and challenge of articulating a vision for or purpose of one's life; as doing so can create immense pressure or stall progress. However, in addition to acknowledging the reflection process as valuable, and the merit of a general guideline and direction that can result, I want to emphasize the importance of having a strategic underpinning for one's path. While I advocate for experimentation and goal-setting, I also believe thinking strategically about what experiments to take on or goals to set is important.

For example, Lou Gerstner speaks in his book about how, in meeting after meeting, he noticed that while the people in the room were extremely bright and committed, there was little strategic underpinning for the strategies and discussions—e.g. customer segmentation and competitive comparisons were not raised.[29] Discussions about vision and strategy must have a solid foundation, a "fact-set," if you will, of the environment within which the organization operates, both externally, with regard to market structure and participants (competitors, customers), and internally, with regard to knowledge, resources, and capabilities. We can then use the facts to ask good questions and think through important considerations for moving forward.

By doing so, we better position ourselves and our companies. Gerstner, for example, acknowledged that "in the face of this

---

29 Ibid.

large global span and uniquely diverse set of customers and an ever-changing technological base, organizing IBM was a constant challenge."[30] But it is hard work that must be done, requiring change through strategic thinking.

And a final lesson from Gerstner. He emphasizes that of all the changes he made in 1993 and 1994 to turn around the company, the most important message he conveyed was the importance of truly working as a team, especially since the chosen strategy centered around integration. Gerstner was not afraid to roll up his sleeves and nearly force communication, sharing of information and ideas, and breaking down barrier to teamwork with IBM.[31]

He was courageous enough to try out different ways to succeed with helping people best work together rather than adhering to the all-too-common phrases in corporate America, "that's just how it's always been done," or "our team isn't responsible for that," or "I have to prioritize my P&L."

Gerstner's story shows that doubt is a powerful force to be used as a tool for self-reflection, understanding, and discovery. After he realized the challenges ahead and truly asked himself whether IBM could lead again, he cites the doubt he had upon accepting the job rush back. Yet, he marched forward, not paralyzed by fear and what came next when figuring things out for the next few steps.

Gerstner just kept moving, asking the hard, good questions and observing while seeking truth along the way. He was

---

30   Ibid.
31   Ibid.

honest and realistic about the mountains to climb and put in the effort. My takeaway from him is to embrace the challenge as something worth pursuing, something worth struggling for, something worth excitement.

AN UNPLANNED LIFE:
KATHARINE GRAHAM'S FALL AND RISE

Among my own generation, recognition of Katharine Graham's name is hit-or-miss. But I think her story is one worth having at least a base level of understanding (and I would encourage reading her autobiography or listening to her own recording of the audiobook).

Graham was the second female publisher of a major American newspaper and led *The Washington Post* for over two decades, including during the Watergate coverage. Her memoir, *Personal History*, won the Pulitzer Prize in 1998. She came from a wealthy family in New York, went to a premier school in the University of Chicago, socialized with the likes of John and Jackie Kennedy, Lyndon B. Johnson, Ronald and Nancy Reagan, Warren Buffet, and other notable people at the time, and yet was not immune to some of the hardest struggles that life can give people.

She had a strained relationship with her mother, who was often condescending, contributing to low self-confidence. Growing up with parents who were rarely home, Graham developed a sense of quiet independence and through university years developed an interest in labor issues. After a short period of working for a San Francisco newspaper, Graham joined the family business, starting work for *The Post* in 1938.

She married Harvard Law graduate Philip Graham in 1940 and had four children.[32]

Her father, Eugene Meyer, handed over the publisher role of *The Post* to Philip Graham in 1946, to which she comments in her autobiography, "Far from troubling me that my father thought of my husband and not me, it pleased me. In fact, it never crossed my mind that he might have viewed me as someone to take on an important job at the paper."[33] Upon Eugene Meyer's death in 1959, Philip also became Chairman of the Washington Post Company and expanded the company with the acquisitions of television stations and *Newsweek* magazine.

Graham's life seemed to be a life filled with success, luxury, and prospects. Except no lives truly are. Philip Graham suffered from alcoholism and mental illness throughout their marriage, often belittling her. He had an affair with an Australian stringer for *Newsweek*, declared seeking a divorce, but then at a newspaper conference in Arizona had a nervous breakdown, was placed in a psychiatric facility, and on August 3, 1963, committed suicide with a shotgun at one of their estates.

His death left the Washington Post Company and *The Post* in Katharine Graham's hands. She became president, publisher and later chairwoman of the board, a role which she held through 1991. Graham became the first female Fortune 500 CEO in 1972 and, despite admitting to sexist biases herself in

---

32 Katharine Graham, *Personal History*.
33 Ibid., chap. 6.

her autobiography, experienced the difficulties of being taken seriously by male colleagues and even employees. She experienced a lack of confidence and distrust in her own knowledge. But with the women's movement gaining momentum, her own attitudes began to change, she began to promote gender equality within her company, after openly making biased, sexist comments against women. She developed, changed, and came into her own throughout her life, not based on a master plan or vision, but by the necessity of circumstances.[34]

Graham's life and story is remarkable, not because of her wealth and the friends she kept, not because of the grand vision she set and accomplished, but rather because of the way she could dynamically take life at each step for what it was. Her life demonstrates the importance of meeting life, and people, where they are (including oneself) in the present, not believing the lies we tell ourselves or others tell us about ourselves, being open to opportunities that arise, and making allies along our journeys.

She confronted her own sexist biases and gave herself grace for her legacy attitudes and dialogue, looking to the future and how she could still have a positive impact on important issues. Not only did she take a more active role in gender equality, starting in her business, but also in communications, once she realized her faults. She applied the same grace to others, meeting people where they were—whether in competency or personal circumstance—rejecting a judgmental approach even after so often being judged, whether for her Jewish background, gender, or knowledge.

---

34 Ibid.

In a perspective-changing story, Katharine Graham was finishing up at a dinner party one evening, a regular occurrence within the circles in which she socialized, where often business and dinner overlapped. When dinner was over, she realized in an epiphany that after dinner it was always expected for the women at the table to move to the parlor together or go to their rooms, whereas the men stayed to discuss "important matters" among other men.

She realized that it is during this time that valuable connections and business topics are discussed, where loyalties are often made, but women did not have a seat at the table, creating barriers that bled into professional life and opportunities. So, she opted to disrupt the natural flow and "took her seat at the table."[35]

While it wasn't necessarily fair for her or other women to be ostracized, it was unlikely to be fixed by men, so she tried to grab the bull by the horns for change herself. This was one of several steps where Graham allowed her own biases and perspectives to adapt and change, dynamic rather than static. She finally refused to believe the great lies that were being told to her about the role of women in business and at home, even the lies she had told herself, and in an interview once.

Like Graham, I, too, have told myself lies about what I can or cannot do, who I can or cannot be. We all do, all too often. It is in the moments of rejecting these lies that we have moments of vision and unlock possibilities, rather than striving toward one grand vision.

---

35   Ibid.

In the same way that Graham acted on an opportunity to break the mold (women heading to the parlor or to bed after dinner), she also did a good job of being open to opportunities that arose. By necessity after the death of Philip, she decided to take on the leadership role of what became a Fortune 500 company. She also took opportunities to meet with and learn from people who might intimidate others, such as Warren Buffett or Lyndon B. Johnson. She sought guidance, listened, learned, and eventually found her voice on various topics. She was okay with the fact that she did not know everything and "just kept moving" in life, despite hardship, doubt, or circumstance, a theme of many people whom we admire in history and the present.

I can relate to periods in her life where she almost seemed unfamiliar or uninformed, but she was comfortable not knowing everything. I grew up with a mother who was a teacher and a father who was an automobile assembly line factory worker. At Michigan Ross, I remember a professor chastised me because "everyone should know what 'FDI'" stands for. I realized that the conversations that my classmates might have been exposed to at the dinner table growing up may have been quite different. Yet on the flip side, like Graham, I appreciate having a sense of freedom from a set of pre-established parameters in life, embracing my ignorance at times with a "sky-is-the-ceiling attitude."

Katharine Graham was not complacent in not knowing everything and saw conversations and meetings as opportunities to learn. By building her expertise, she became more impactful in her role and garnered the trust of her colleagues. She built her own confidence, which later became pivotal with the

Pentagon Papers decision. To do so, Graham sought out and openly took in outside guidance, such as that from Gloria Steinem, but stayed true to her beliefs, even as those evolved.

One final characteristic that benefited Graham was the strong ability to make allies. Despite her lack of confidence in herself and her knowledge, she befriended Warren Buffett and cultivated his financial advice. He became a major shareholder of her company—he had confidence in something about Graham.

This is one of several examples where she could have shied away from conversations or responsibilities outside her area of knowledge, but instead she asked questions, sought knowledge from others, and as a result made allies through her genuineness. Some of us may naturally make allies more easily than others do, but anyone can take steps to engage others and learn about someone's interests, what book they are reading, and how life is going for them.

Katharine Graham lived a long life, becoming a notable American, woman, publisher, and leader. Her story, however, was not filled with rainbows and unicorns. More and more, I am convinced our stories never are. That is the beauty of life. Graham experienced many struggles in life from the death of a spouse to career issues; her story shows an example of an iconic success of emergence. Each chapter of her life led to a relatively unplanned next chapter. She was in some ways "pulled" through life, so she had to decide at each step how to react, what outlook and attitude with which to approach life, and whether to learn and change or not.

* * *

On December 30, 2018, I started reading Gerstner's book while on a train to the Blue Mountains outside of Sydney, Australia. It was rather ideal timing, as I was reflecting on New Year's resolutions and what lay ahead in 2019. What I had been thinking a lot about was where I thought my career was going. Growing up in Michigan, I was naturally interested in the automobile industry. And the consulting firm I worked for and was going back to after business school primarily served manufacturing-heavy industries in the United States, from chemicals to automotive to industrials.

Over the next few weeks, Gerstner's story gave me confidence in knowing that big, well-established companies, like IBM, face disruption from competition and technology. I was able to envision how going back into these industries after graduate school provided a unique opportunity. Reading Gerstner's book while taking a class on innovation, I realized that a career path I could get excited about lay in consulting for industries ripe for disruption, leading them and advising them through a new era of design and innovation.

Like Gerstner, I don't necessarily have a master plan for accomplishing this, but I see the issue and can "just keep moving" toward this ambition. And like in my Grand Canyon adventure, I cannot do it alone, which means making allies and leaning on others along the path.

Graham's story actually became my running rhythm for some time. When training for a marathon in the winter and using treadmills primarily to do so, you need to plan your content for your long runs. And listening to Katharine Graham's audio book, narrated by Mrs. Graham herself, was my music. When I heard her convey her pain through life's tragedies, my own pain, my burning lungs, my tight hamstrings didn't seem so bad. Because the truth is, people are incredibly resilient. And Graham stayed open to opportunities, asked questions with a real desire to learn, and made allies despite her challenges.

Both Lou Gerstner and Katharine Graham faced immense personal and professional challenges. But they are now known as notable leaders who effectively had an impact on history. How might their stories strike hope in you? What is the next mountain you'll climb or canyon you'll conquer? And how can Gerstner and Graham's tactics guide your path? I continue to be inspired by both of their stories and the impact they had.

CHAPTER 5

WHEN VISION EMERGES

Every time you are tempted to react in the same old way, ask if you want to be a prisoner of the past or a pioneer of the future.

—DEEPAK CHOPRA

In many ways, the stories I have written about—Katharine Graham's rise as a wife, mother, widow, CEO, and life-long learner; Lou Gerstner's unexpected entry into the computer and technology industry; Brenner's intrigue for, exile from, and rekindled love for chocolate; SurePayroll's survival; and Shackleton's return from the edge of the world—all have elements of emergence within them. Our lives and the world change, whether by driving forces in technology, dynamic decisions of people, or otherwise. Inevitably, what happens next in any story has an element of surprise and the unknown. Otherwise, life would be far less interesting.

However, an important concept I want to try to highlight through a few other stories is the power of the pivot. When life, purpose, or vision pulls you along—call it destiny, fate, higher power, or chance—knowing when to pivot and when not to changes the frame of possibility. Moreover, being in a state that is open to and aware of opportunities for a pivot is important; those who successfully pivot have commonalities that anyone might try to adopt.

A SWERVE: LET'S MOVE! CAMPAIGN AND WHERE IT ALL BEGAN

The first story of a master "pivoter" comes from a very well-known woman in the United States, new author and former First Lady Michelle Obama. In Michelle's autobiography, *Becoming*, she tells the story of her life up until 2018. She delves into her childhood, recounting the small second-floor apartment her family rented from her aunt, the neighborhood kids she played with, and the poor schooling circumstances from which her mom saved her. These and other accounts from Michelle's childhood and early adulthood point to how, by whom, and where she grew up had a profound impact on her values, knowledge base, personality, and psyche.[36]

Living in a small apartment where her parents lived paycheck-to-paycheck, in a neighborhood where it became less safe to play outside, and seeing her father's health deteriorate over time, led Michelle to appreciate stability, structure, and following a plan, overall appreciating the management of risk and following point A to point B to point C.

What she did not expect, and what we all know, is that she would one day meet a disheveled, rain-drenched, and late law

---

36 Michelle Obama, *Becoming*.

intern who would turn her world upside down. Despite being dissuaded by some of her high school teachers about setting her sights too high,[37] Michelle attended Princeton University from 1981 to 1985, majoring in Sociology and minoring in African-American Studies. She then moved to Boston and graduated with her Juris Doctor from Harvard Law School in 1988.[38]

The teachers who in high school discouraged Michelle from reaching her potential were planting lies. Lies that would seed doubt in Michelle about her capabilities and what she might be able to one day do and accomplish. Katharine Graham had been told lies about the role of women at home, in the workplace, and in after-dinner discussions. She not only internalized these and conformed but also, self-admittedly, spread the lies until she learned otherwise.

For Michelle, she was told lies about her race, her gender, her socio-economic status, her intellectual prowess and competence, and likely much more. The moment she embraced her identity as "both brilliant and black" at Harvard and in subsequent years, Michelle began to peel back truths, not believing the lies others had told her and she had told herself.

Upon graduating from Harvard Law School, Michelle began building her career, working on marketing and intellectual property law for Sidley Austin LLP in downtown Chicago. One summer, a new summer associate, Barack Obama from Harvard Law School, stumbles in, drenched and late reporting

---

37   Valerie Strauss, "What Michelle Obama Told High School Students."
38   "Michelle Obama Biography."

for his first day and his meeting with his informal associate buddy, Michelle Robinson. The pair eventually became a couple and, as Michelle and Barack's relationship grew, so too did their aspirations.

Michelle characterized Barack as more care-free and adventurous, and herself as more structured and a plan follower. But knowing Barack and taking a liking to some of his perspectives on life prompted Michelle to consider *not* climbing the law firm ladder. Michelle Obama began building strong relationships and developing opportunities in Chicago city government, the non-profit sector, administration at the University of Chicago's student services, and later in administration of the University of Chicago Hospitals through part of Barack's 2008 primary campaign. The First Lady role fell into her lap because of her husband and, as we know, First Ladies have a certain expectation to support an initiative. Michelle took the role even further, with the hope of truly going after a major public health issue in our country, childhood obesity and nutrition.

Neither Michelle nor anyone else could have predicted this, but Michelle pivoted from one doubt and opportunity in life to the next. And when life asked her the question about whether to climb the law ladder or not, she "swerved." Barack served as a catalyst for her thinking beyond the norm certainly, but Michelle through deep reflection at each step stood up to the task at hand, unafraid of lack of knowledge or experience. She took meetings and built relationships. She tried something out and then something else.[39]

---

39 Michelle Obama, *Becoming.*

What we learn from Michelle is to look ourselves in the mirror, ask ourselves what our values are, imagine what our life might be like if we make one decision or another, and not be afraid to "swerve" and walk through door number three. Her story also teaches us something more subtle—in a love partnership, sometimes one partner's "moment" may take precedence. This can cause resentment, conflict, and even relationship failure in some cases. Yet one can feel some of these things and choose to make the most of it, adapting and finding meaning despite one's owns goals being somewhat deprioritized, as Michelle did with her Let's Move Campaign around childhood nutrition. And through her hard work, she will become one of the most influential and impactful First Ladies to push the boundaries of what is possible, beyond expectations, for the role.

FROM SPANISH BANKERS TO FOOLISH DISCOVERY
From one University of Chicago dean to another, the manner in which the world's first executive MBA program expanded internationally provides a story that highlights how opportunities can emerge and how following breadcrumbs can lead down interesting paths.[40] Professor Harry Davis joined the faculty of the University of Chicago Booth School of Business in 1963, was deputy dean from 1983 to 1993, and continues to teach today. While Harry's roles at Chicago Booth have changed over time, he currently serves as a professor, teaching two courses to hundreds of students each year, Strategy Lab and Business Policy.[41]

---

40 "How the World's First Executive MBA Program Changed Business Education."
41 "Harry L. Davis."

Many stories, no, many books in fact, could be written about Harry's adventures, from his alter-ego, "Runway Harry"—who keeps three magazines about things he doesn't know with him to open up on airplanes to strike up conversations with those he sits next to—to his pioneering the first core leadership program of any top-rated MBA institution in the country. However, I want to tell a story about Spanish bankers and royalty in a far-away land.

One framework within Harry Davis's repertoire on strategy and leadership is "Harry's Creativity Habits." And number six of seven habits is to "Put a few surprises on my schedule." During his tenure as deputy dean of the Chicago Booth School of Business, Harry asked his administrative assistant to "put a few surprises on his schedule." These could be having a palm-reader come in, taking a walk, or something else that was intended to be relatively unknown and unplanned by Harry.

One week, Harry saw an hour-long meeting description on his calendar that read "Spanish bankers." Harry thought that certainly this was some code, a funny description of some fun "surprise" on his schedule, and had nothing to do with either Spain or bankers. So shortly before the meeting, he asked his assistant what he should do or where he should go. To which she relayed this was an actual meeting with Spanish bankers.

While Harry was somewhat confused, he obliged and took the meeting where Spanish bankers proposed that Chicago Booth open a satellite location for the school in Andorra, a small country between France and Spain. After the meeting, Harry wrote an email, paraphrasing, "thank you, but no thank you," ending the email with a paragraph that could have been argued to leave the door open, but this was only included out of courtesy, not as a hint to continue.

When Harry was in Europe on a business trip for the school, his assistant asked if he could swing by Andorra because the Spanish bankers had followed up, not taking the "thank you, but no thank you" hint. So, somewhat annoyed by the persistence of these men, he acquiesced and visited Andorra while on a trip to London and Brussels. Again, he wrote a "no thank you" email in January of 1991.

In July of the same year, Harry had an unscheduled visit to Barcelona. While there, he visited one of the famous Spanish architect Gaudi's buildings. He went out on the building terrace and saw the view. He could not ignore a question as Spanish bankers came to mind: "why not?" Why couldn't Chicago Booth have a physical educational presence in Europe? This is when the idea for an executive education program in Barcelona was born, an executive program that could serve European executives through high flight-traffic through Barcelona and enhance overall brand awareness of the school in Europe, a long-term play in attracting talented students and networks around the world.

After this artistic moment on a terrace in Barcelona, Harry took out some paper and wrote at the top "Concept Statement: A Castle in Spain," then below, "What is it? How will it work?" Instead of doing what he had done for months, thinking about why it wouldn't work and writing "thank you, but no thank you" emails, he flipped the script and started to imagine it.

As consideration and evaluation of the idea progressed, Harry Davis was told there was "no market in Europe" by a hired consultancy. Despite this and his own hesitations early on, his curiosity, sense of imagination, openness, and ability to ask how it could work resulted in the first time an executive MBA program expanded internationally. Davis didn't stop there; he became part of the solution by going and teaching at the new Barcelona location.[42] At present, Chicago Booth has moved its European footprint to London and has a footprint in Singapore, as well, building upon the learnings and starting point in Barcelona.[43]

In his 2019 Convocation Remarks for the executive MBA graduation, Professor Davis remarked:

"Being foolish is most often associated with mistakes, bad outcomes or someone's shortcomings. . . . The French actor and director Sacha Guitry once opined: 'Our wisdom comes from our experience, and our experience comes from our foolishness.' I recently ran across a three-line poem titled "Naïve."

- *Do you ever want to be naive?*
- *Yearn to be in those moments when you were foolish*
- *Before knowledge tainted our innocence?*

A foolish idea for starting a full-time MBA program in Andorra was brought to me in 1990 by three visitors whom I had never met. I am the fool now standing before you who found a silly excuse to take a side-trip to Andorra three months later to continue this foolish conversation. He never

---

42 Harry Davis, "Competitive Advantage," (session three).
43 "How the World's First Executive MBA Program Changed Business Education."

dreamed that with the help of many people, there would now be campuses for our Executive MBA Program on three continents. A question for leaders, then, is when does foolishness hurt and when does it help?"[44]

Harry taught me that sometimes foolishness can lead to learning opportunities or bring forth intriguing ideas or actions, sparking curiosity. In addition to letting oneself be curious, having a sense of imagination, and being open, this story illustrates how sometimes strategy emerges rather than being intentionally crafted.

So, the question is, do we write "thank you, but no thank you" emails every time, or do we leave some doors open and walk through others? Like many students who hold an MBA from Chicago Booth, I was fortunate to be a student of Harry's—and for me a two-time classroom student and lifelong learner—while earning my MBA from 2017 to 2019. This story of Harry's, as well as many others, led me to be more open to things within my own life, such as moving outside the Midwest for the first time when a door opened.

JOINING THE SANDBOX OF UNCERTAINTY
"To infinity and beyond," one of the most famous phrases from one of many people's favorite childhood movies, Toy Story, actually came from one man's story of adventure. Ed Catmull, co-founder of Pixar, had a dream to create the first computer animated film.

---

44 Harry Davis, "Keynote Speaker."

Early in life, Catmull had a vision of becoming a film animator, even animating using flip-books. However, once adulthood was eminent, Catmull took physics and computer science at the University of Utah instead of pursing the movie industry. His first roles after his undergraduate degree were at Boeing in Seattle and then at the New York Institute of Technology before returning to Utah for graduate school in 1970.

While in graduate school, Catmull revisited his interest in animation under Ivan Sutherland and with a talented and highly motivated group of graduate students. Catmull recounts in his book: "Professor Sutherland used to say that he loved his graduate students at Utah because we didn't know what was impossible."[45] Sutherland had a computer drawing program that Catmull was able to experiment with and his vision to create the first computer animated film took a strong hold.

As life is prone to do, however, after earning his doctorate in computer science, Catmull's roles took him on a wandering path from 2D and 3D computer graphics to Lucasfilm, working more on digital editing then animation. Even after Steve Jobs bought Lucasfilm's digital division, founded Pixar in 1986, and made him the chief technology officer, Jobs pulled Catmull away from animated film creation initially, toward commercializing the Pixar Image Computer for government agencies and the medical research community. Pixar came close to losing support or being sold to another

---

45 Ed Catmull and Amy Wallace, *Creativity Inc.: Overcoming the Unseen Forces That Stand in the Way of True Inspiration*, chap. 1.

studio due to slow progress, but eventually Catmull and the team created one of the most successful and loved films of our time, *Toy Story*.⁴⁶

After realizing his dream of creating the first computer animated film with *Toy Story* in 1995, Catmull was left with a sense of loss: "I couldn't deny that achieving the goal that had defined my professional life had left me without one. *Is this all there is?* I wondered. *Is it time to find a new challenge?*"⁴⁷ What was his purpose now? Should he leave Pixar? In the difficult year after the debut of *Toy Story*, he felt compelled to redefine at least a new guiding principle.

Eventually, Catmull iterated on his reflections and set a new goal: to build an organization that could continually produce magic long after he and the other Pixar cofounders were gone. He wanted to "protect Pixar from the forces that ruin so many businesses,"⁴⁸ which gave him renewed focus. Later in his book, *Creativity Inc.*, Catmull talks about change, randomness, and what's hidden, followed by "The Unmade Future" in chapter eleven.

He describes randomness through his experience of being in just the right place during a car accident in his childhood; he might not even be standing today. He uses many examples to drive home that randomness and how what is hidden from us (what could have happened but did not) plays a role in outcomes.

---

46 Ibid.
47 Ibid., Introduction.
48 Ibid.

In "The Unmade Future," Catmull emphasizes that we never know what might happen in life, so while we can have goals and experiment, life is inherently the "sand box" of uncertainty in which we play. This shows value in having goals, i.e. ideas and things to play with, while taking life in stride as we are sometimes lucky and other times unlucky. We should not bury our heads in the sand so as to miss emergent opportunities, but we can also have a sense of humor when luck strikes out, as it sometimes will.[49]

In an interview with McKinsey's Allen Webb and Stanford University professors, Catmull gives an analogy about why Pixar's rule of making a great movie requires a strategy of experimentation and pivoting:

"Think of building a house. The cheapest way to build it is to draw up the plan for the house and then build to those plans. But if you've ever been through this process, then you know that as the building takes shape, you say, 'what was I thinking? This doesn't work at all.' Looking at plans is not the same thing as seeing them realized. Most people who have gone through this say you have to have some extra money because it's going to cost more than you think. And the biggest reason it costs more than you think is that along the way, you realize something you didn't know when you started.'"[50]

Catmull's story, and how he redirected his goals, is really about sustainably freeing up creative impulses within a team, through practices and culture and leadership

---

49   Ibid., chap. 11.

50   "Staying One Step Ahead at Pixar: An Interview with Ed Catmull."

philosophies. And a significant piece of doing so is embracing mistakes as important building blocks of invention and innovation.

As Professor Sutherland appreciated, at least pretend or convince yourself that you do not know what is impossible. Another important piece is having a goal, reaching it, riding it out or moving on, anticipating or experiencing decline, and resetting. Catmull was once quoted: "That's what I try to express in the book. . . . Pressing reset is what we've been doing over and over again. That is what you do. Because as soon as you make 'making it easy' a goal, then you've really messed things up."[51]

It is critical to acknowledge that Catmull gained confidence in saying no and being relentless when something would not align with a goal or work toward the ultimate good of the goal. These characteristics are evidenced in Catmull's decisions, from declining an on-paper attractive theme park ride-design role, to refusing to let Disney resources and Pixar resources be shared after the acquisition, to name only a couple of examples. While adapting and being open to life's emergent opportunities is important, showing discipline in pursuit of a goal is important, as well. To me, Catmull exemplifies getting the balance right, leading him to have led a successful career with Pixar. He played with ideas, adapted along his path, and had major impact where he valued it most, which was with his employees and with his audiences.

* * *

---

51   Chris Bell, "Pixar's Ed Catmull: Interview."

These stories about having the courage to swerve in a comfortable life, choosing to keep a door open, and playing in the sandbox of uncertainty is where I am in life right now. I think many people are in a similar situation. What I find incredibly powerful about them is that it's where the magic happens, should we choose to be okay with the uncertainty and ambiguity.

Growing up in a suburb between Detroit and Ann Arbor, Michigan, I was lucky to grow up with family. On a sixteen-acre plot of land sat four houses: my parents, two sets of aunts and uncles, and my grandmother. Now, these four houses still stand, and within a twenty-minute radius live all their children and grandchildren on my mother's side—except me.

After graduating from the University of Michigan, I moved about an hour away from the family property and traveled four days of the week out of state for my consulting work. In my field of business, a common question after a few years of experience is whether to obtain an MBA. I knew it would position me well for the future and saw the need to grow as a business leader, so I wanted to do it. But I had already attended the best business program in the state for my undergraduate degree.

So, I pondered, *should I attend a local school, maybe going part-time, or do I go back to Michigan Ross for my MBA, or do I explore options outside of Michigan?* No one in my family had a business background, so I sought career advice from colleagues. Their encouragement was more toward gaining a new, different experience. And that's what I did, attending one of the top MBA programs in the world at the University of Chicago Booth School of Business.

This decision took me to Chicago, but I always intended to move back to Michigan—until I moved to Chicago, found that it was easy to still visit Michigan, and enjoyed what a new place with new people had to offer.

And I could not help but think, *If I move back to Michigan now, I'll probably never leave.* So the low-risk choice was to stay put in Chicago.

Until I met Leon.

Leon was from everywhere—he would have been born in the Philippines had a volcano eruption not been imminent, and then moved around growing up as a military kid. From Washington, DC, to Alabama, Alaska, Florida, Arkansas, Pennsylvania, and Illinois, Leon was used to moving around.

At this point in the book, you know that Leon has become my graduate school love story. From meeting in Colombia on spring break, to hiking the Grand Canyon together, to ringing in 2019 by the Sydney Harbor bridge in Australia, to running a marathon together, Leon and I have grown close. And in this love story, Leon's career prospects from graduate school were going to take him to New York City.

And despite being a girl who had always planned to stay in Michigan, I had to decide. Do I swerve?

I now live in New York City, by Rockefeller Plaza in Midtown. Never did I think I would live in New York, where people were brash and busy and bumped into on the street.

And I love it. The music, the art, the theater, the parks, the food—oh, the food!

While I don't know where my journey will take me, and I do miss Michigan and the proximity of family, I realized my life is mine to build. So, I decided to swerve, to keep doors open, and to play in my sandbox.

PART THREE

WRITING YOUR VERSE

CHAPTER 6

RESOLVING VISION

The highest levels of performance come to people who are centered, intuitive, creative, and reflective — people who know to see a problem as an opportunity.

—DEEPAK CHOPRA

Up until now, what I have laid out are stories of people, past and present, with musings of their futures, who have gained some sort of notability. In each case, this notability may or may not have grown from a vision or intentional purpose that has anything to do with his or her current state or landing point in life. My commentary was meant to be primarily observational but inherently laid the foundations for what I am trying to convey.

Regardless, throughout and henceforth, I want to dive into some questions:

- Why do many of today's most successful people say that their life "emerged" or was built day-by-day?

- How can anyone adopt similar emergence or self-discovery principles to best position for what he or she would be satisfied with at the end of life?

What I am proposing in this book is that success, or being satisfied at the end of life, is less about achieving an established vision and more about what one might say about you in your obituary someday. And specifically that we, at any time, in my estimation, can play an active role as a participant in writing that story without adhering to a set vision or purpose statement.

If doing so is particularly difficult for you because you do not feel led toward or attracted by something, do not feel stuck. Rather, read on. When vision goes wrong, when lack of vision goes right, when pivots are necessitated or chosen, embrace change and uncertainty, experiment often, and learn humbly.

FACILITATIVE MANTRA: EMBRACE CHANGE— EXPERIMENT OFTEN—LEARN HUMBLY

The stories I've told or touched on—Santiago in *The Alchemist*, SurePayroll, Ernest Shackleton, Max Brenner, Lou Gerstner, Katharine Graham, Michelle Obama, Harry Davis, Ed Catmull, and several of my own—all have something "impressive" about them—taking on a difficult feat, succeeding against the odds, and so on. But all of them also noted failures, too. Regardless, these stories provide an impressive slate of experiences by their protagonists.

Their lives and notability are predicated by just that, a slate. Multiple slates. And having many different experiences and perspectives requires change. And change should not be feared, but rather embraced as a part of our development and crafting of the book of our own lives. There are many chapters, many pages. There are plot twists, there are tragedies. The question is whether we will take up the pen and write, and with what will we fill the pages?

* * *

Pixar's *Up* would be described by critics as a heartfelt adventure impeccably crafted with wit and depth. But in *Creativity Inc.*, Ed Catmull reveals the extent to which the film changed during its development. One might not even recognize today's *Up* in the early and even mid-term scripts. In fact, only two things survived the original screenplay script: the title and a bird character.[52]

Pete Docter, who directed *Up*, highlights that change is important and failure, too, in the process. "It wasn't until I finished directing *Monsters, Inc.* that I realized failure is a healthy part of the process," Docter said. Catmull reflects, "the path Pete followed on *Up* was difficult and unpredictable; there was nothing about where the movie started that indicated where it would end up. It wasn't a matter of unearthing a buried story; in the beginning, there was no story." Pete drove home the point, "If I start on a film and right away know the structure—where it's going, the plot—I don't trust it. . . . I feel like the only reason we're able to find some of these unique ideas, characters, and story twists is through

---

52 Ed Catmull and Amy Wallace, *Creativity Inc.: Overcoming the Unseen Forces That Stand in the Way of True Inspiration*, chap. 8.

discovery. And, by definition, 'discover' means you don't know the answer when you start."[53]

Catmull himself said, "I've known many people I consider to be creative geniuses, and not just at Pixar and Disney, yet I can't remember a single one who could articulate exactly what this vision was that they were striving for when they started. In my experience, creative people discover and realize their visions over time and through dedicated, practiced struggle. In that way, creativity is more like a marathon than a sprint. You have to pace yourself."[54]

And change and uncertainty is inevitable, so one might as well embrace it. When I read this part of Catmull's book, I had an existential moment of clarity, as I was training at the time for my first marathon run. I didn't know what would happen the day of my first marathon on March 17, 2019, in Asheville, NC. I hoped to finish the run, but I had heard stories of tight hamstrings, rolled ankles, and more happening during the run itself. All I knew was I could keep practicing. I had to have a vision for reaching the vision line, put in the work for training, and take one step at a time.

The notion that change is a positive thing and helps our stories be written every day, with every job and every plot twist in our lives, and that we can take an active role in creating change in our lives, may be an uncomfortable thought. And it may make us feel like an imposter, or inauthentic, but it's necessary.

---

53   Ibid.
54   Ibid., chap. 11.

Herminia Ibarra, professor of leadership and learning at INSTEAD, remarks in her article, "The Authenticity Paradox: Why feeling like a fake can be a sign of growth,"

"In my research on leadership transitions, I have observed that career advances require all of us to move way beyond our comfort zones. At the same time, however, they trigger a strong countervailing impulse to protect our identities: When we are unsure of ourselves or our ability to perform well or measure up in a new setting, we often retreat to familiar behaviors and styles. But my research also demonstrates that the moments that most challenge our sense of self are the ones that can teach us the most about leading effectively. By viewing ourselves as works in progress and evolving our professional identities through trial and error, we can develop a personal style that feels right to us and suits our organizations' changing needs."[55]

Change will happen anyway, and rather than be a passive observer where changes only ever happen to us, why not be an active participant, intentionally inviting change and having a seat at the screenplay writing table as our plot is written? Therefore, I suggest to actively experiment, often. And do the work to learn from your experiments, humbly.

In this last part of this book, I want to present several frameworks, tactics, and thought exercises for groups and individuals to employ to invite change in through experimentation, reflection, and learning. But first, to summarize some of my key learnings from the stories told before:

---

[55] Herminia Ibarra, "The Authenticity Paradox."

TAKEAWAYS TO EMBRACE CHANGE, EXPERIMENT OFTEN, LEARN HUMBLY

1. Don't believe the lies you tell yourself; among others, Katharine Graham's life demonstrates the importance of meeting life, and people, where they are (including oneself) in the present, not believing the lies we tell ourselves or others tell us about ourselves, being open to opportunities that arise, and making allies along our journeys.

2. Just keep moving: there is value in separating movement from direction, like being able to get a car out of the snow—back and forth movement, BEFORE changing direction. For me, getting in the habit of exercise, I hired a trainer, saw little results on the scale, but created "movement," then the direction happened (forty-five pounds lost!).

3. Stay curious: read a lot, ask questions, never say "this is how we've always done it." Most people don't have extraordinary or exceptional success because they didn't develop their opportunity field, not because they didn't develop their skills/capabilities.

4. Treat life as art, not science: in "The Secrets to Designing a Curiosity-Driven Career," Zainab Ghadiyali, who works as a product lead at Airbnb and co-founded Wogrammer, said this: "When you look at a painting from a distance, you see a larger, cohesive picture. But as you approach the canvas, you see that there are, in fact, hundreds of separate strokes that make up that picture. Think about your career as a work of art—expansive, independent movements that

incrementally reveal a whole."[56] Ms. Ghadiyali's words resonate with the examples of SurePayroll, Michelle Obama, Katharine Graham, and Ed Catmull.

5. "Expect the tiger to be tricky" mindset: Ed Catmull says, "In the context of animation, directors have told me that they see their engagement when making a film as extremely active. It seems like it's good psychologically to expect these movies to be troublesome. . . . it's like someone saying, Here, take care of this tiger, but watch your butt, they're tricky. I feel like my butt is safe when I expect the tiger to be tricky."[57] He also noted, "Taking a risk necessitated a willingness to deal with the mess created by the risk."[58] Sometimes our choices in life come with pleasant surprises but can also come with unpleasant consequences. Regardless of which results, however, learning is guaranteed, so embrace the tiger.

6. Make allies: like Katharine Graham, know that even if you are not the most knowledgeable person in the room on a topic, you can learn from others and be supported by your allies. So, make them! Seek out relationships with people you admire, have a different perspective or set of experiences, and/or who you enjoy being around.

7. Process experiences: in *Creativity Inc.*, Catmull describes: "'We should be careful to get of an experience only wisdom that is in it—and stop there,' as Mark Twain once said, 'Lest

---

56 Zainab Ghadiyali, "The Secrets to Designing a Curiosity-Driven Career."
57 Ed Catmull and Amy Wallace, *Creativity Inc.: Overcoming the Unseen Forces That Stand in the Way of True Inspiration*, chap. 7.
58 Ibid.

we be like the cat that sits down on a hot stove-lid. She will never sit down on a hot stove-lid again—and that is well; but also she will never sit down on a cold one anymore.' The cat's hindsight distorts her view. The past should be our teacher, not our master."[59] We go through our lives often consuming experiences. Experiences are undigested. But learning from our experiences comes from processing them. Writing a book, an essay, keeping a journal—these are ways to process. There are certainly many others.

8. Set the intention, not the outcome, from the start. Before a difficult conversation, remind yourself why you are having the conversation. And when things don't go your way, reframe situations to not see oneself as a victim but rather a student to learn.

9. Get to know yourself: utilize self-awareness and reflection tools and techniques as datapoints, not fates.

10. Be relentless: Catmull declining the theme park job. My training on Saturday nights for a marathon. Have an idea of what you believe in or the impact you want to have (maybe not who you want to be), like Steve Jobs believing in "really great products."

At the same time, be aware of the following: imposter syndrome and competing priorities. Imposter syndrome is common language used by young professionals these days. It is when an individual doubts their accomplishments and fear being exposed as a fraud.[60]

---

59   Ibid., chap. 9.
60   Gill Corkindale, "Overcoming Imposter Syndrome."

I would encourage such people to reframe the situation as best as they can, thinking of the opportunity to try something where at least someone, even if it is not themselves, sees potential for them. Taking a lighter approach to vision and purpose helps with this "imposter syndrome" trend.

Catmull, for example, would sometimes ask a group of leaders and managers he was addressing, "'How many of you feel like a fraud?' And without fail, every hand in the room shoots up." He said, "The trick is to forget our models about what 'should' be."[61] He goes on to talk about managing others well, but I think the point applies to managing ourselves.

Regarding competing priorities, life's busyness and our own commitments can lead to other people's agendas becoming our own. I would suggest being gracious with oneself and others, not being selfish per se but making known one's priorities and expectations. It is important to pour from a full cup, which happens when one's pursuits and priorities are in fact prioritized overall. While both the imposter syndrome and competing priorities are natural and will happen with regularity in life, they can be acknowledged, managed, and reframed so one is not permanently distracted from self-discovery or blinded to emergence.

LOOKING AHEAD

What resonated strongly with me in Catmull's book is his proposition that the value of a mental model (frameworks,

---

61   Ed Catmull and Amy Wallace, *Creativity Inc.: Overcoming the Unseen Forces That Stand in the Way of True Inspiration*, chap. 6.

tactics, metaphors, practices) is it enables whoever uses it to get what they want to get done, whatever that may be, done. "What's essential is that each of us struggles to build a framework to help us be open to making something new. The models in our heads embolden us as we whistle through the dark. Not only that, they enable us to do the exhilarating and difficult work of navigating the unknown."[62]

What I have done thus far is establish some patterns from the stories told up until now, the observations and principles of these successful navigators of change, randomness, and life. What I want to do going forward is present a collection of frameworks, tactics, and practices—mental models, if you will—for teams and individuals to experiment with, reflect on, and make their own. The intent is to promote ideas for one to find what might work for them, and if nothing else to provide some to try, such that anyone can become an expert navigator of their own journey, discovering and writing life along the way.

Before moving to the next chapter, I'll leave you with this story from Ed Catmull:

"Not long after I arrived, she sat down in my office and presented me with a two-year plan that laid out exactly how we should manage various staffing issues going forward. The document was specific about targets we would reach and when we would reach them. It was meticulous. . . . so I was gentle when I told her it wasn't what I wanted. To show her what I wanted, I drew a pyramid on a piece of paper. 'What you have done

---

62   Ibid., chap. 11.

in this report is to assert that in two years we will be here,' I said, putting my pencil lead at the top of the pyramid. 'Once you assert that, though, it's human nature that you will focus only on making it come true. You will stop thinking about other possibilities. You will narrow your thinking and defend this plan because your name will be on it and you will feel responsible.' Then I started drawing lines on the pyramid to show how I'd prefer she approach it."[63]

He goes on to represent having a goal in mind but re-assessing learnings and progress every few months, resulting in an end which is different and perhaps better than originally envisioned. Catmull shows that having a plan is not a bad thing, but what he taught here is that the plan should leave room for learning. The following chapters highlight practices that are not meant to be plans but rather to facilitate the mantra: *embrace change, experiment often, learn humbly.*

---

63   Ibid., chap. 12.

CHAPTER 7

FRAMEWORKS AND PRACTICES FOR THE GROUP

—

The capacity to learn is a gift; the ability to learn is a skill; the willingness to learn is a choice.

— BRIAN HERBERT

Since several of the stories I have told relate to teams and organizations, and much of our lives are dedicated to one or more companies, I'd like to touch on some frameworks to consider in the context of groups or teams, whether work or in one's personal life. These frameworks aim to promote progress, learning, and creativity.

Two companies, Google Ventures and Pixar, offer specific practices that promote trying things, playing with ideas, and getting feedback. All of these are important to change, experimentation, and learning. While they cannot be fully explained in a short overview, my intent is that a brief description along with reference resources will be helpful for future exploration.

DESIGN SPRINT

Jake Knapp is now a self-employed writer, soon to be publishing *Make Time: How to Focus on What Matters Every Day.* He is the acclaimed, New York Times best-selling author of Sprint: *How to Solve Big Problems and Test New Ideas in Just Five Days.* A "sprint" is "a simple step-by-step system for improving focus, finding greater joy in your work, and getting more out of every day."[64] While Jake describes the development of a "sprint" mostly within the context of Google, his experiences as a designer at Oakley and Microsoft certainly influenced his build-out of the practice at Google.

The process is now a tried-and-true application of design thinking, a process for human-centered, creative problem solving, that aims to reduce risk quickly when bringing a new product, service, or feature to the market, or to management within a company. Sprints aim to stop the "old defaults of office work and replace them with a smarter, more respectful, and more effective way of solving problems that brings out the best contributions of everyone on the team—including the decision-maker—and helps you spend your time on work that really matters."[65]

---

64 Jake Knapp and John Zeratsky, *Make Time: How to Focus on What Matters Every Day.*

65 "The Design Sprint."

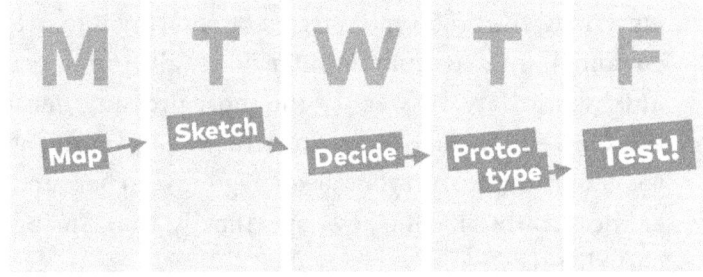

Image credit: https://www.thesprintbook.com/how[66]

As the graphic above shows, a sprint is a relatively quick way to structure ideation over the course of a work week, Monday through Friday.

- On Monday, the team works to "map" out the sprint week through a series of structured conversations.
- On Tuesday, each member of the team creates a "sketch," or a detailed, opinionated solution for the problem identified on Monday, following a four-step process that emphasizes critical thinking.
- On Wednesday, the stack of solutions from Tuesday go through a five-step "Sticky Decisions" method to identify the best solutions and create a storyboard, a step-by-step plan for your prototype.
- On Thursday, the team builds a realistic prototype of the solutions in the storyboard to simulate a finished product for customers. The philosophy of Design Sprint prototyping is about "fake it 'til you make it" by simulating a finished product for your customers that allows you to have something realistic for testing on Friday, optimizing learning potential through data collection.

---

66 Ibid.

- On Friday, the prototype is tested by showing it to five customers in five separate interviews, aiming to get quick-and-dirty answers to the most pressing questions. An entire guide on how to actually run a sprint at your company or with your ideation group can be found at thesprintbook.com/how, specifically the "Spring checklists (PDF)."[67]

While conducting a design sprint for a product idea that I had, I learned there were sufficient workarounds and that my product was not getting at a problem people care about. Through prototyping and talking with customers, I learned there were plenty of other steps to solve before my product idea would become relevant. By going through a design sprint, I de-risked the next step by focusing on assessing product-market fit and built value as the product idea was tested and refined through user input.

In a conversation with the founder of BioVenture Advising, a biotech startup, on August 3, 2020, Stephanie Wisner spoke about her work in science startups as building value (and the startup valuation) by conducting experiments. Experiments are conducted in these startups to produce data sets that provide companies with the data they need to assess the results of the drug. Each experiment produces a data set which provides more evidence for the drug and more instances to analyze effectiveness. Success for science startups is often to build enough value to be acquired by a pharmaceutical company; thus, the data and evidence in building the valuation is critical. I think conducting a design sprint is similar in the

---

[67] Ibid.

sense that data and input is gathered, usefulness is assessed, and value is built.

The principles and methodology of Knapp's Design Sprint could also apply to personal problem solving. Why not think about something you are trying to solve or something you want to explore for self-development? You could develop a pseudo-design sprint during which you try potential solutions and de-risk your next steps. In the next chapter, I describe a personal framework for experimentation that I use. At the core, my framework shares similarities with a Design Sprint.

BRAINTRUST AND POST-MORTEMS AT PIXAR

In *Creativity Inc.*, Ed Catmull writes: "While experimentation is scary to many, I would argue that we should be far more terrified of the opposite approach. Being too risk-averse causes many companies to stop innovating and to reject new ideas, which is the first step on the path to irrelevance. Probably more companies hit the skids for this reason than because they dared to push boundaries and take risks—and, yes, to fail. To be a truly creative company, you must start things that might fail."[68]

At Pixar, Catmull helped set a tone as a leader of embracing change, experimentation, and learning. Two experiments that became regular practices to facilitate dialogue and progression are braintrusts and postmortems.

---

68   Ed Catmull and Amy Wallace, *Creativity Inc.: Overcoming the Unseen Forces That Stand in the Way of True Inspiration*, chap. 6.

A braintrust is a group of trusted colleagues that get together periodically to review the progress of a Pixar film that is in development: the characters, the story, and the design. During these gatherings, colleagues are expected to be very openly thoughtful and critical, even if they do not have a recommended solution for an observed issue and even if the comment is just "this feels off."[69]

The discussion might be about the overall story or a clip of the film that is shown during a meeting. Pixar's *Up* went through many iterations in story due to the braintrust and resulted in a highly-acclaimed film. Catmull says that the essential ingredients for conducting a successful braintrust include "frank talk, spirited debate, laughter, and love."[70]

The Incredibles went through a braintrust meeting in which the participants did not feel quite right about an argument between Mrs. Incredible and Mr. Incredible. In the scene, Mr. Incredible came across very much like a bully, which was not the intention. The group identified the false intent here and, after the director and artists went back and tried different things, they found a way to change the feeling of the scene. It was not until the artists physically made Mrs. Incredible bigger in size that the bully-like tone of the scene was resolved.[71]

Here, the braintrust identified that something wasn't working. And in the end, there was no change to the dialogue; rather,

---

69 Ibid., chap. 5.
70 Ibid.
71 Ibid.

they just had her stretch to be bigger. Regarding the braintrust, Catmull writes in *Creativity Inc.*: "Its most important characteristic was an ability to analyze the emotional beats of a movie without any of its members themselves getting emotional or defensive."[72]

Any team, company, or individual could do something similar. Imagine showing a piece or the full story of a work presentation, thinking of it like a story or film and inviting trusted colleagues to shape the communication and quality of analysis based on the data evidence and knowledge of the industry or problem. Or imagine a group of tenth-grade teachers having a braintrust around lesson plans. Or a team of retail store employees having a braintrust to discuss store layout and customer service practices.

At the individual level, imagine seeking input from either trusted friends or colleagues, or even from trusted acquaintances who can provide an unbiased view about your personal development and goals. When I was applying to graduate-level business schools, I received a piece of advice from a work colleague to identify two people I could trust but who don't know me that well. I was advised to do mock-MBA interviews with them to see if my MBA story and examples made sense to people who did not know them already. Even for a personal goal, a pseudo-braintrust enabled best practices to be shared, feedback to be given, and progress to be made.

Another practice at Pixar is the postmortem. Too often in workplaces, once a meeting is conducted, a presentation is given, or

---

[72] Ibid., chap. 4.

a report is submitted, the team that prepared it does not come back together to discuss, debrief, and seek learnings. Often, there is pressure on our capacity, as our time at work is required for the next project or task, resulting in wrap-up, knowledge management, and learning to be rushed or skipped. Postmortems help groups reflect and process a route into understanding ways that the team or work was exceptional and ways that the team or work was not exceptional.

Ed Catmull described the first postmortem at Pixar in 1998 after finishing *A Bug's Life* in *Creativity Inc*. A timer was used to ensure that no one person spoke too long. The team took an entire day to delve into all aspects of the production. In retrospect, no "aha!" moment came from the meeting, but everyone was engaged in rethinking how things had been done and learning from errors.

It became a practice that, by even scheduling it, forced participants to reflect and come prepared. Catmull reflected that perhaps ninety percent of the value of the postmortem came in the preparation. And the output arms people with good questions to raise on the next project to best frame the project. Again, a postmortem could also be used to learn at a personal level—about one's annual goals, career decisions, relationships, or personal endeavors, like a personal Design Sprint or experiment.

To help guide preparation, the high-value piece according to Catmull, the leader or facilitator can ask everyone to make two lists for the meeting: the top five things they would do again, and the top five things they wouldn't do again. Catmull cites using this practice as a key success factor.[73]

---

73   Ibid., chap. 10.

By providing instructions for preparation, the postmortem discussion proves to be particularly useful because the preparation was manageable in terms of time requirements and straightforward. Consequently, the output can be consistently talked about and aggregated. Postmortems or something like them are not profound by being new—but they are profound when practiced well.

For example, postmortems in health care do not reach value potential because only cases that go wrong are under evaluation. Conversely, at Pixar, postmortems are conducted for all films, not just those that did more poorly at the box office. Postmortems done well then consolidate what has been learned, are able to teach others who weren't there, prevent resentments from festering (because they are addressed), compel reflection, and pay it forward (future films reap the benefits of learning from prior mistakes).

JUST KEEP MOVING

Having covered frameworks used at Pixar, it would only be appropriate to transition to my final group framework through the words of beloved Pixar character, Dory, in *Finding Nemo*: "Just keep swimming." Sometimes, our teams or ourselves are barely above water, or perhaps even feel as though we are sinking. This is where a specific strategy if chosen can be born—when there is no other option.

At the University of Chicago Booth School of Business, Professor Harry Davis offers four meta-perspectives on the "how" of strategy. There is a system-level view and unit-level view, and one of the system-level view meta-perspectives is "existential," a strategy with no real options. In this system-level view, as opposed to a system that is evolving, where you can change and adapt, *just keep moving*.[74]

Do something, take some step or action to avoid getting stuck. The path forward may not be clear, but chances are, one small step will find its way down an interesting path.

In his classroom, Professor Davis recounts an example of a woman who went from liking to cook to leading the catering for a major airline company in Chicago by making small forward movements, even in the face of adversity and no real options. She was willing to take a step, even if it was not what she originally might have dreamed (becoming a restaurant chef, for example). And she ended up learning something about herself—that she cared most about helping people through her passion for cooking, and that the platform can change to still do that.[75]

In another example, recall the story of Lou Gerstner, the CEO who turned IBM around in the 1990s. He actually stated to the press and the investor community soon after he started that "we don't need a vision." Yet Gerstner went on to lead IBM through another heyday period and is viewed as a legend. He said what he said about vision because he emphasized early, "We don't need a 'vision' right now . . . we just need to keep moving."[76]

---

74 Harry Davis, "Competitive Advantage," session three.
75 Ibid.
76 Louis V. Gerstner, Jr., *Who Says Elephants Can't Dance?*

The last part, "keep moving," was often dropped in the media uproar at his words. But he conveys here that, sometimes, it is not the right time to set a strategy or a vision but rather take actions to address key issues within the business to better operate. Again, we see the importance of taking small steps to move forward and the value in doing what needs to be done, even if it is in the weeds.

Any company or individual can adopt the existential strategy if it is deemed appropriate. Of course, we must be aware of competitive actions and understand the scenarios and risks associated with this strategy in a changing landscape. But a perhaps sexier grow-through-acquisition approach might not be appropriate before an existential strategy of addressing key issues within the business so it can better operate, and so future acquisition and integration can perhaps be more valuable.

* * *

The frameworks and practices described above—design sprint, braintrust, postmortem, and existential strategy—are not my own by any means, but are tried and true practices of companies that have gone on to experiment, create, innovate, and succeed in ways that were meaningful to them. I believe there are lessons here that can be adapted and applied at the group level or individual level.

Given advances in technology and rising trends, I would expect to see more companies thinking hard about how to best increase their capacity to be nimble and increase creativity and innovation within their businesses. Sprints, braintrusts and postmortems, and existential strategy are three methods to experiment with to enhance learning and new ideas. While each of these strategies are implemented in the business world, they can easily be used when trying to break out of your comfort zone and embracing change. In the same way, I am convinced new approaches that companies develop will also be leverageable for personal growth and development.

CHAPTER 8

FRAMEWORKS FOR THE INDIVIDUAL

―

The most creative act you will ever undertake is the act of creating yourself.

―DEEPAK CHOPRA

After a physical therapy appointment for my sprained ankle in spring of 2019, I was walking through Chicago's Millennium Station when, to my annoyance, there was a group of kids and chaperones taking up the width of the hallways and walkways of the station. As I squeezed through, I heard one adult tell a child, "Don't let ten seconds of your day ruin your day." This was twenty or so minutes after my physical therapist said, "Life is ten percent what happens to you; ninety percent what you do about it." My ankle sprain was the result of a misstep off some steps, halting my running progress for six-to-eight weeks.

This lesson to the child is one we should tell ourselves often. Things in life will happen―we will lose promotions or jobs, relationships, our health, and more. But what do we choose to do next? This is where strength of character and rigor of discipline come in. I have found three specific personal frameworks to be profoundly helpful in changing the frame of what to do next as an individual and to experiment with what one brings to the table: Professor Robert Quinn's Fundamental State of Leadership, Professor Harry Davis's Stage Page, and my own simple framework of Quarterly Experimentation that I call the Experiment Experience.

FUNDAMENTAL STATE OF LEADERSHIP

To navigate life's many uncertainties, I find Robert Quinn's Fundamental State of Leadership (FSL) framework extremely helpful. The framework balances keeping an end in mind while also processing new information and situations. The FSL framework provokes a person to ask four questions in any situation, whether in an interaction with another person or a situation in which a decision needs to be made:

1. Am I being results centered?
2. Am I internally directed?
3. Am I others focused?
4. Am I externally open?[77]

These questions promote imagination while staying grounded in results orientation, embracing our ability to play an inductive role in our own lives. In his book, *Moments of Greatness: Entering the Fundamental State of Leadership*, Professor

---

77 Robert E. Quinn, "Moments of Greatness: Entering the Fundamental State of Leadership."

Robert Quinn provides a comparison between the different elements of the framework[78]:

In the normal state, I am...	In the fundamental state, I am...
Comfort Centered	Results Centered
I stick with what I know.	I venture beyond familiar territory to pursue ambitious new outcomes.
Externally Directed	Internally Directed
I comply with others' wishes in an effort to keep the peace.	I behave according to my values.
Self-Focused	Other Focused
I place my interests above those of the group	I put the collective good first.
Internally Closed	Externally Open
I block out external stimuli in order to stay on task and avoid risk.	I learn from my environment and recognize when there's a need to change.

Image credit: https://sbdctampabay.com/four-steps-great-leadership-character/

So how does this align with "Embrace change, experiment often, learn humbly?" By going through the simple question framework, we are opening ourselves up to and inviting the possibility for change, experimentation, and learning. And by trying out this framework alone, you are experimenting. Quinn suggests that intention, integrity, subordination, and adaptability are core dimensions that make up the state.

Take a simple example: imagine walking into a business meeting between sales and IT where a major mistake was quoted to a customer. If I am director of sales and have a relationship with that customer, I am likely upset on many levels and have to make hard decisions going forward: do I honor the quote and not reap the financial benefit that would have flowed to the business and to my variable compensation? Do I work with the customer on a new quote blaming IT? Or something else? And what do I do in the meeting with IT? Do I start blaming and explaining the

---

78 Ibid.

many ramifications for the mistake which, from my perspective, was IT's fault in mislabeling a field in the online portal? Do I jump straight to demanding IT relabel the field? I can, instead, take a step back and walk through the Fundamental State of Leadership.

1. Am I being results centered? Both IT and sales have an interest in the right quote getting to the customer in the best way. Let's see if we can agree in the meeting on that intended result.

2. Am I internally directed? Even though my boss, the head of sales, expects me to give IT a lashing for mislabeling the field, hoping to prevent anything like this from happening again, I strongly value reconciliation and relationship-building. Knowing that "giving a lashing" will harm the relationship with IT, I will approach the conversation form a direction of reconciliation and growing stronger in our working relationship from this misstep.

3. Am I others focused? Though this mistake will inevitably cost me time (and possibly money) in the long run, coming up with a way to address the situation as it stands in a way that works for everyone, and coming up with a better way of working in the future, is in the best interest of the company. Communicate this and earn the trust and respect of all in the room.

4. Am I externally open? Being willing to listen to IT first and foremost may yield high returns. There could be an underlying issue that has been left neglected, whether in

standard processes, compatibility across departments, or the system itself. Rather than getting defensive, both marketing and IT can try to acknowledge what's really going on—even if it means suggesting to management a dramatic change.

While I provided a business example above, I have personally used FSL in many personal situations, from a conversation with my sister to a disagreement with my boyfriend. If there is a decision or conversation that you anticipate, whether personal or professional, I encourage you to take a few moments to walk through the Fundamental State of Leadership framework.

More often than not, you walk out doing the unexpected, disarming whoever might have had hostility or defenses up. This diffuses a situation to the point where clarity of thought can be realized, and progress can be made. And, by practicing the framework when you can anticipate a need (in advance), I have found my ability to act according to its principles "in the moment" far easier—this is the "state" of the Fundamental State of Leadership that Robert Quinn developed. We can enter and exit it, certainly. It can be easy to enter any time, which takes practice.

THE STAGE PAGE

Professor Harry Davis of the University of Chicago Booth School of Business teaches his students a framework for personal agility based on Barbara Lanebrown's "The Stage Page Tool." He describes a performance stage, for a play, for example. There are stage directions that refer to different areas of the stage: downstage is on the stage and is closest to the audience; upstage is on the stage but farther from the audience; and offstage, perhaps in various areas, are not seen by the audience.[79] See below:

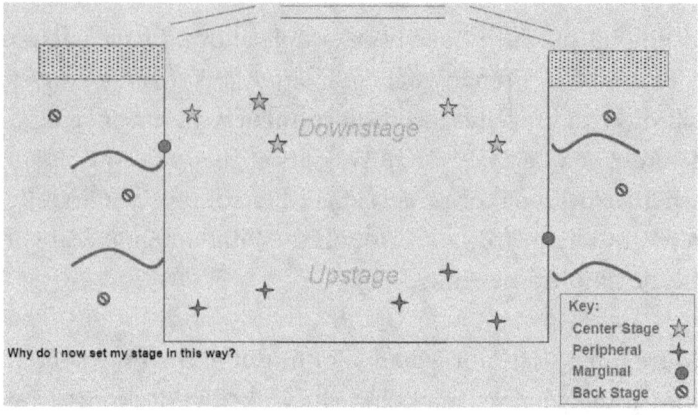

Image credit: p 18 http://www.morassociates.com/2008conf/HarryDavis-ITLeadershippdf.pdf

What the Stage Page Tool does is utilize the stage as an illustrative set for the various "characters" we can play in life, suggesting that "the way in which someone relates to the outside world and to themselves is greatly influenced by the position of characters on stage. The tool also emphasizes that characters are not inherently "good" or "bad," in that a character with a seemingly negative connotation can be useful, or what we would ascribe as "good," in the right circumstance. For example, being "aggressive" can be very useful in certain situations. What's important is identifying when to leverage each character.

---

79 Harry L. Davis, "Leadership as Performance Art."

The "characters" fall on stage as follows:

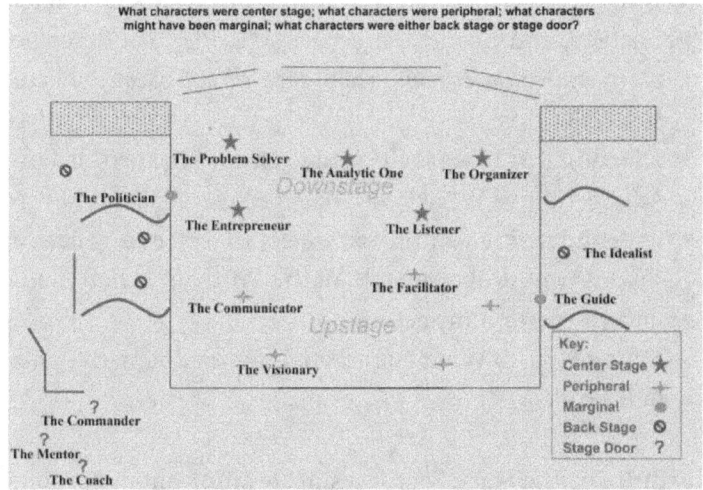

Image credit: p 19 http://morassociates.com/2009conf/2009conffiles/Davis-ITLP-Conf-2009.pdf

An intended practice conducted by those who use the Stage Page Tool is to plot one's current characters on the Stage Page (see the example). Then, over time, in new roles or as one wants to experiment, move the characters around, add new ones, take one off. Most importantly, think about what might happen if you do any of these, try it, and reflect on what you learn.

Professor Harry Davis also prompts his students to conduct creativity experiments using the Stage Page Tool, using diagnosis and action planning as follows:

- Diagnosis: 1) Select a "character" that I want and need to bring on stage or move downstage to increase creativity in my work and/or life.

- Diagnosis: 2) What is my motivation for accessing or repositioning this character?
- Diagnosis: 3) Current Script: *If* I bring this character onstage, and/or move it downstage, *then* . . . describe the negative outcome(s) that you would expect to occur if you did this.
- Diagnosis: 4) What is the source of this "If/Then" belief?
- Action Plan: 5) What low-risk experiment(s) could I run over the next two to three weeks in order to generate disconfirming evidence about this "if/then" belief? (audience? situation? my action?)
- Action Plan: 6) What quantitative and/or qualitative data will I collect?[80]

By utilizing the Stage Page, we start to think about how our personal traits, elements of our personality in some way, are flexible, or at least perhaps explorable. We start to experiment with our ceilings, and we start denying the lies we or others have told about what we can do, who we can be, and where we can go.

The Experiment Experience

The last individual framework is my own. It's quite simple, and many people have forms of the same thing, but it is something that I have formalized for the purposes of personal accountability and consistency.

One source of inspiration for me in creating this framework and using it regularly in my life comes from Pixar's

---

80 Harry Davis, "Competitive Advantage," session four.

Ed Catmull and his approach to leadership. Pixar has a designated institution for learning called Pixar University, P.U. Catmull says, "the purpose of P.U. was never to turn programmers into artists or artists into belly dancers. Instead, it was to send a signal about how important it is for every one of us to keep learning new things. That, too, is a key part of remaining flexible: keeping our brains nimble by pushing ourselves to try things we haven't tried before."[81] He goes on to express how children learn so much so quickly and are open to do so because everything is new to them, so they have no choice but to embrace the new. They have no fear, love surprises, and are all the better for it.

My framework is a way to help me and others perhaps not lose that childlike openness as adults. Catmull wrote regarding creativity, "In Korean Zen, the belief that it is good to branch out beyond what we already know is expressed in a phrase that means, literally, 'not know mind.' To have a 'not know mind' is a goal of creative people. It means you are open to the new, just as children are. In Japanese Zen, that idea of being constrained by what we already know is called 'beginner's mind.' And people practice for years to recapture and keep hold of it."[82] This idea is, in my own view, important to self-discovery, as our lives are truly "created" every day.

---

81 Ed Catmull and Amy Wallace, *Creativity Inc.: Overcoming the Unseen Forces That Stand in the Way of True Inspiration*, chap. 10.

82 Ibid.

My framework, the Experiment Experience, is about conducting specific "experiments" in a time-bound manner followed by reflection each quarter of the year (January through March, April through June, July through September, and October through December). When I first started using this framework in the third quarter of 2018, I looked at it more like goal-setting. Being in my fifth iteration now over a year later, I find I think of the "goals" more like "experiments." At first, I did not have a long-term vision or overarching goal in mind. Rather, I was truly just trying to incorporate regular progress toward independent goals into my life, because working sixty-to-ninety hours per week resulted in doing little for myself outside of work. But now, the roots of these goals are starting to be woven together toward my drafted vision statement—and work is part of that. I want to make the different parts of my life work together, rather than against each other, in terms of time demands, and this framework helps me organize myself.

My mindset is this: I commit to trying three things with specific parameters around what "trying" means within the next three months. The goal is to try them, the experiment is to see how it goes. So think of them as goals or experiments, whichever makes the most sense for you. At the end of that set of three months, I assess 1) whether I successfully "tried" it, 2) what happened, 3) what I learned, and 4) think through what I want to do next, if anything, about that experiment—i.e., make it a part of my normal life, never think of it again, or somewhere in between.

I also build in buckets, or categories, to force diversification and well-roundedness. However, in one quarter, July through

September of 2019, two of my three experiments were in the same category. And that's okay—the categories, nevertheless, create mindfulness over time about your key areas of focus. My categories are 1) Mental/Cognitive, 2) Physical, 3) Emotional/Spiritual, 4) Relational, and 5) Skillful. And really, the framework is that simple.

One of my early "cognitive" experiments was "read (start and finish) a book about entrepreneurship" to see if I wanted to rekindle reading in my life, which I have, while exploring a space I wanted to learn more about. For physical, I have completed the following experiments: did yoga weekly in Q3 of 2018; ran a marathon in Quarter 2 of 2019; learned how to play tennis in Quarter 3 of 2019. For spiritual, some of my experiments have been to read daily devotionals, listen to sermons while I run as much as possible (staying current on sermons from three churches, one in the Detroit area, one in Chicago, and one in New York City). For Relational, I started weekly get-togethers in Quarter 2 of 2019 with a group of ladies from business school to savor (quite literally over brunch or dinner) our last few months together before graduating from business school. For Skillful, I obtained a motorcycle permit and took a motorcycle riding class in Quarter 2 of 2019. While I did not end up getting a license, I thoroughly enjoyed learning how to ride.

These experiments were far more powerful than I expected, as they often led to learning about a new interest, meeting interesting people, and/or gaining a broader perspective. What has been particularly interesting is seeing how seemingly disparate goals come together, as connections between interests are made. For example, learning that I love to run and relate to people through service has made me want to start a running ministry through church in the future, relating my spiritual, physical, and relational interests. I see this as having potential for impact in my draft vision statement about glorifying God by using my strengths in ideation and pragmatism to bring structure and action to abstract thought, helping people and companies change for the better. In this sense, I can use my methods for going from being able to jog less than a half mile before wanting to get sick to finishing a marathon to help someone bring discipline, health and fitness, or a new hobby to the person's life.

Below is a simple structure to conduct each quarter of the year. I encourage you to write this down somewhere, keep a journal or a tracker.

STRUCTURE FOR THE EXPERIMENT EXPERIENCE: FIVE STEPS

1. Set Three Experiments
2. Conduct Them
3. Reflect
4. Catalog Your Learnings
5. Prepare to Repeat

STEP 1: SELECT THREE EXPERIMENTS

- Select three experiments, whether mental/cognitive, physical, emotional/spiritual, relational, skillful, or otherwise
- Ask "why did I choose this experiment?"
- Ask *If* the outcome of the experiment is X, *then* [brainstorm ideas insights, results, or feelings]

- Ask "what might occur that could create unexpected outcomes?" How do I think I will feel? How do I want to react to a new course?
- Ask "what are my next steps?" Is there data to collect, planning to be done, a training plan to put on my calendar? Should I tell people for accountability?

STEP 2: CONDUCT THEM
- Try to track against your plan
- Collect your data if applicable
- Schedule what you need to

STEP 3: REFLECT:
- Acknowledge actions taken, missteps, and/or drivers of wins
- Identify failures and successes, accept them, and process them
- Recognize the people who played a part and in what ways

STEP 4: CATALOG YOUR LEARNINGS:
- Ask "what insights did I gather?"
- Brainstorm whether/why it matters
- Foster dialogue with others about what I can take away
- Fill in your journal or template with your learnings

STEP 5: PREPARE TO REPEAT
- Think through whether to extend or change a previous experiment

- Take inventory of the categories that you are most prone to conduct experiments in and those you avoid. Do you want to change the balance, or not?
- Consider how you can stretch yourself through the next experiment

When conducting these experiments, I have identified a couple critical success factors in completing the experiments and getting the most out of them. Similar to the idea of having allies like Katharine Graham, I suggest developing a support network. Tell someone or multiple people about your experiments. They can serve as a partner in doing some of them, a coach or mentor if they have previous experience, or simply a cheerleader.

In addition, if one of your experiments is to run a marathon, one of my personal examples, or write a book, another of my personal examples, you're going to have to create a training or writing plan. I recommend doing this with any goal or experiment. It is a transforming perspective to look at everything like running a marathon. You have a vision (getting to the finish line) but there is a lot that needs to be done and learned to get there (training). You're going to have to practice or prepare. And you're also going to have to adapt. e.g. an injury, busy schedule, etc. Put blocks on your Google, Outlook, or Planner calendar to carve out dedicated time to ensure you actually do the experiment.

To be sure, I am not saying that individuals, teams, or corporations should only ever experiment. I can see how this can come across as being fickle, non-committal, or flaky. If a commitment is made, follow it to the best of your ability and/or confront the need for change head-on with yourself and those affected and involved with such a change. If responsibility is held, carry it.

I can also see how this can be perceived as not oriented toward results, driving toward desired outputs and outcomes. However, this framework can be used to explore or to provide structure in working toward a desired result. In either case, the goals or experiments are the inputs into how you may choose to craft your life.

In the case that a purpose or vision has been defined, this framework can be used to explore ways to get there, de-risking the approaches through rapid experimentation and building value through the learnings of the experiments. In business, this is similar to design thinking and the concept of rapid prototyping to identify a solution for an identified problem. What is of utmost importance in this approach is driving toward finding product-market fit, the sweet spot where the solution concept is positively accepted by the market (customers/users). In the same way, the Experiment Experience enables those who use it to map out a path toward a vision.

* * *

To close this chapter, I want to recall a brief story. The story comes from a short book called *The Little Prince* about a crash-landed pilot meeting a boy prince in the middle of the desert from another planet. The main theme of *The Little*

Prince is the importance of looking beneath the surface to find the real truth and meaning of a thing.[83]

There is a fox character who teaches the prince to see with one's heart instead of just with one's eyes. The fox tells the boy, "And now here is my secret, a very simple secret: It is only with the heart that one can see rightly; what is essential is invisible to the eye."[84] The fox explains that one becomes responsible for what one has tamed, and the prince realizes that he is responsible for the rose on his planet—that while it came with responsibility, the boy tamed the rose and has a responsibility to it.

The prince conveys to the pilot that, unfortunately, most adults have difficulty seeing with the heart, which inevitably calls for a sense of openness to adventure, while maintaining a sense of responsibility.[85] The frameworks and practices in this book chapter—the Fundamental State of Leadership, the Stage Page, and the Experiment Experience—offer ways to reconcile these. We can aim to be curious, exploratory, and adventurous with our lives every single day, while honoring commitments and having an end, or vision, in mind.

The Fundamental State of Leadership helps us navigate decision-making along our path. The Stage Page helps us think through the most effective way to move along our path, managing interactions along the way. And the

---

83   TheBestNotes Staff, "TheBestNotes on *The Little Prince Study Guide*."

84   Antoine de Saint-Exupéry, *The Little Prince*.

85   Ibid.

Experiment Experience helps us stay curious to what the best path is by breaking down the next steps into time-bounded efforts. Whether used in tandem or individually, these frameworks have helped me become more mindful, open to change, and, to be honest, more interesting through engaging experiences.

CHAPTER 9

TECHNIQUES TO RESET EXPLORATION

The worst curse to befall anyone is stagnation, a banal existence, the quiet desperation that comes out of a need for conformity.

Research has shown that the best way to be happy is to make each day happy.

—DEEPAK CHOPRA

The last two chapters have given overviews of frameworks, practices, and mindsets that both groups and individuals can use to spur exploration, reflection, and learning. All of those are meant more for ongoing use, integrating them on a somewhat regular basis into one's life. But sometimes, we have "regular basis" overload. We need to eat, sleep, exercise, date, pray. . . . fill in the blank on a "somewhat regular basis." And that can be exhausting. So, I'd also like to offer some tactics one might use as a one-off effort to reset exploration or inspiration.

What if we find ourselves in a rut, doing the same thing, day-in and day-out? We see the same people, get exposed to the same sorts of articles and podcasts, work on the same task. And we just need a short, compartmentalized way to have a change. Several actions I will briefly explain that are or were practiced by the people whose stories I talked about in Part Two of this book, or from other interesting people I've met along my own journey.

TAKE A RETREAT WITH AN INTENTION

Consider taking a reading retreat or a silent retreat. A reading retreat is a way to "get away" for a weekend or a few days and to explore something of interest, something new, or just to indulge in fiction. One professor whose course I took at the University of Chicago Booth would take a few books for a long weekend by herself.

Generally, these books would all be on *different* topics. For example, one might be about fiction, one about business/management/leadership, and one about someone or something she doesn't know anything about. Her rationale in this is that creativity and innovation is often spurred by the recognition of patterns between diverse ideas or the ability to make connections between diverse ideas.

In a brief anecdote, Steve Jobs used to drop in on classes at a local college or university and through this learned about calligraphy. He eventually made the connection between text on a computer screen and calligraphy, and fonts were born.[86]

---

86 Matt Rosoff, "The Only Reason the Mac Looks Like It Does Is Because Steve Jobs Dropped In on a Course Taught by This Former Monk."

An alternative to a reading retreat is a silent retreat. Pixar's Ed Catmull did this grudgingly, prompted by his wife, almost quit multiple times, but found the introspection useful. He contemplated the concepts of control, change, randomness, trust, and consequences, leading ultimately to a clear mind through silence and mindfulness. He was able to focus on ideas without getting caught up in plans and processes. His learning was to make peace with what we cannot control and be open to new ideas and to deal with our problems squarely.[87]

Reading retreats and silent retreats give us the time and head space to play with ideas, to think about new things, and to just remove ourselves physically from "normal." While an epiphany may not come, such intentional retreats (as opposed to a vacation retreat) often spur change, experimentation, and learning after returning to "normal" through a renewed and inspired mind, body, or spirit.

TAKE A SHULTZ HOUR

Another practice that one can adopt on a whim, either once or repeatedly, is taking a "Shultz hour." In the image below, George Shultz shares a moment with Ronald Reagan in Ireland in 1984.[88]

---

87 Ed Catmull and Amy Wallace, *Creativity, Inc.: Overcoming the Unseen Forces That Stand in the Way of True Inspiration*, chap. 11.

88 David Leonhardt, "You're Too Busy. You Need a 'Shultz Hour.'"

Image credit: https://www.nytimes.com/2017/04/18/opinion/youre-too-busy-you-need-a-shultz-hour.html Michael Evans/White House/The LIFE Images Collection, via Getty Images

George Shultz is the former director of the United States Office of Management and Budget, United States Secretary of Treasury, dean of the University of Chicago Graduate School of Business, United States Secretary of Labor, business executive at Bechtel, member of multiple boards, and informal advisor in multiple capacities. With a body of incredibly demanding roles and responsibilities, Shultz established for himself the "Shultz hour."[89]

Once each week, Shultz would take a pen and paper and an hour and ask himself something like, *What are we trying to do around here? What's our strategy?* Then write. Only the President or his wife could interrupt this protected time.[90] What if more people did something like this? And why can't we?

---

89 Mike Sturm, "The Shultz Hour."
90 Harry Davis, "Learning from Experience/Doing the 'Right' Thing," session nine.

In 2017, The *New York Times* published an opinion article where David Leonhardt wrote: "You're Too Busy. You Need a 'Shultz Hour,'" which emphasizes that the busiest people could glean the biggest benefits.[91] And specifically, shape the idea according to your needs—what you ask yourself might be different, like "What am I grateful for this week?", "What do I like learning about?", "What am I curious about?", or "What do I do in this position at this company at this time to make a difference?" And we can keep asking ourselves these questions at different Shultz hours. There doesn't need to be an outcome or grand insight that comes out of the practice, but it is the act of taking a step back that can ground and inspire us.

TALK TO HUMANS

In contrast to taking a silent retreat but in the same vein as a reading retreat, a person can *talk to humans*. In marketing and entrepreneurship, wisdom suggests the importance of understanding your customer.[92] Who is your target customer? What are they like—their likes, dislikes, habits? If you provide a prototype of a project, do they use it in the way you intended, and how do they use it in ways you did not necessarily intend? What are their motivations and drivers in decisions? Do their beliefs match their actions? Ultimately you, as the marketer or entrepreneur, are trying to uncover how to increase the chances a person will buy, and perhaps buy frequently, what you're selling.

---

91 David Leonhardt, "You're Too Busy. You Need a 'Shultz Hour.'"

92 Giff Constable, "Talking to Humans: Success Starts with Understanding Your Customers."

In my MBA course, "Strategic Leadership in Management Networks," research pointed to the value of being a "broker" in networks, where a "broker" is essentially a person who is connected to multiple clusters of people and information, such that he or she is able to "broker" information and relationships from one cluster to another.[93] By talking to humans, you are inherently putting yourself in the position to be exposed to information and to gain access to new or different clusters. Then, ideas from one cluster can be experimented with in other clusters, creating opportunities to explore, experiment, and learn. Take the opportunity in "talking to humans" to be inspired from what others are doing. Be lifted out of a funk and try something different.

GIVE A "LOLLIPOP"

Drew Dudley, billed as one of the most inspirational TED speakers of all time, and founder and chief catalyst at Nuance Leadership, Inc.,[94] gave a spirited talk at *TEDx*Toronto in 2010 called "Leading with Lollipops." As he describes it, a "lollipop" is a moment when someone said or did something that you feel made your life fundamentally better.[95]

Part of discovery, inspiration, change, and learning is about the role other people have had in your life and where you are today. With reflection, we can think about what moments have fundamentally made our lives better. And we can remember *who* a driver for that moment was. And most importantly, we can let them know.

---

93   Ron Burt, "Brokerage," session two.
94   "196 – Drew Dudley: Found & Chief Catalyst of Nuance Leadership Inc."
95   Dr. Lynda, "The Power of Giving People a 'Lollipop Moment.'"

Dudley emphasizes this practice as "everyday leadership," acknowledging the smaller moments in life, rather than letting the big things overwhelm us.[96] In resetting discovery and exploration, we can be inspired by the acts of others who have helped us in life and think about how we might do this for others. With this mindful awareness of the difference that one person, one moment can make, we are encouraged to appreciate small things, inspiring the next small thing. Take rest in the small things, be grateful, and be at peace with where you are today and what has gotten you there. And if need be, make peace with anything holding you back from doing so.

BE YOUR OWN "RUNWAY HARRY"

In Chapter 5, I talked about Professor Harry Davis's role in launching the first international executive MBA program. But I also alluded to his self-described alter-ego, "Runway Harry."[97] Professor Davis promotes having a healthy curiosity and appetite to expand our awareness and knowledge base in life. One way to do this is by coupling learning about something totally new to you with being open to it catalyzing a conversation with someone, perhaps even with a total stranger.

Professor Davis's "Runway Harry" practice is to take three magazines about things he doesn't know much about with him to open and read on airplanes to strike up conversations with those he sits next to. At worst, he reads a bit about something he knows nothing about, and his curiosity is sparked, or he learns that he is or is not interested in that topic. At

---

96 "TEDxoronto – Drew Dudley 'Leading with Lollipops.'"
97 Harry Davis, Business Policy.

best, a total stranger sitting next to him notices the magazine, asks something like "Do you have a motorcycle?", and conversation ensues.

Harry recounted one example where, on a trans-Atlantic flight, the conversation lasted over ten hours and birthed a friendship that has lasted ten years. This practice breaks several social norms perhaps, like trying to have a conversation with a stranger on an airplane, but Harry cites many learnings and moments of inspiration.[98] What can it hurt, after all, to open the door, listen, and see what can happen? Anyone could do this; buy a few magazines and take one or more with you on the subway, plane, or at a coffee shop. And see what happens.

DREAM IT UP IN A WORLD OF IMPOSSIBILITY

One of the most valuable pieces of feedback I received a couple years into my management consulting career was "Dream it up even if you don't know if it exists or is possible." My project manager at the time and I were discussing how best to think about a problem and model it out in Microsoft Excel.

She encouraged me in this microcosmic moment not to let my knowledge or lack thereof with Excel hold me back from structuring in my mind the best model to give the best information to inform the problem at hand. She said to first dream it up. THEN, we would look for steps to take or things to try to make it work. And in this case, it was likely my lack of knowledge of the full capabilities of Microsoft Excel that was limiting the dreaming.

---

98 Ibid.

As a result, I started to sketch out my model structures on paper, with bullets outlining what I wanted the model to do (analysis-wise), what I wanted it to show, and how I wanted to use the information. Then, I would leverage the information we are fortunate enough to have at our fingertips through Google. I would also ask colleagues about how to most efficiently and effectively build the functionality to make it work.

I think this example is illustrative of a mindset we can adopt to create a healthy relationship with uncertainty. If we have an idea of what we're interested in learning about, things we're curious about, or the sandbox we want to explore, we can create a structure or frame within which to explore—such as my creation of my three experiments per quarter structure in the Experiment Experience framework.

CREATE YOUR OWN

If none of these practices resonates or you want to keep exploring possibilities, I would encourage anyone to think about their own best-practice tactics. One way to provoke such is to ask the people in one's life whom you admire (or an individual whose work and/or life you respect) what practices they have used or use currently that helps them reset exploration and inspiration.

Not only might this result in a body of ideas, but also it helps you understand someone whom you admire or respect just a bit more. Then try one or more of them. Perhaps try one and then, a week or two later, try another. Experiment through your experimentation. Ultimately, have fun, and play with the ideas of change, experimentation, and learning.

CHAPTER 10

ETHICS AND VISION

In a person's career, well, if you're process-oriented and not totally outcome-oriented, then you're more likely to be a success. I often say, 'pursue excellence, ignore success.' Success is a by-product of excellence.

—DEEPAK CHOPRA

The last three chapters provided ideas on how to embrace change, experiment often, and learn humbly through various practices of discovery, exploration, and experimentation within groups and as individuals. In this last chapter, before providing some ending thoughts and concluding, I would be remiss not to touch on the concept of having principles, even if one does not have vision or purpose explicitly defined.

I would argue that adopting a mindset of adaptable purpose through experimentation frees you to keep a high moral standard. One's ethics no longer become secondary to the requirements demanded by a grand purpose or vision. Rather, one's guiding principles can be a moral measure against which to think through decisions.

GUIDING PRINCIPLES

In addition to a mantra of openness—embrace change, experiment often, learn humbly—the stories I have studied suggest that expert navigators of emergence and discovery adhere to implicit or explicit guiding principles. In the book *Principles*, Ray Dalio discusses fundamental truths that serve as foundations for behavior in work and in life. He argues that "to be principled," means to consistently operate with principles that can be clearly explained.[99] These are akin to thinking about core values, deciding what you want to be true of you, what is true of you, and what you should do to achieve the first in light of the second. Writing down these principles can help structure thinking and clarify them.

These principles can then serve as criteria under which to make a decision or take a position at work or at home. For example, recall the film *Wallstreet*: Bud Fox, a junior stockbroker at Jackson Steinem & Co. in New York City, wants desperately to work for Gordon Gekko, a famed Wall Street businessman. In his desperation, Bud gives Gekko inside information, which leads to a series of unethical requests for information and spying by Gekko. Deceit, greed, and guilt lead eventually to Bud Fox's arrest for insider trading.[100] What were Mr. Fox's principles in this matter? Imagine if his core moral fiber was woven with the principle of integrity rather than greed—how would the outcome have been different? The vision or intent was

---

99   Ray Dalio, *Principles: Life and Work*.
100 *Wallstreet*.

irrelevant—one's principles can be guideposts no matter the decision or situation.

Early on, Ray Dalio developed criteria for decision-making in taking a position in the markets. Upon closing out a trade, he could reflect on the efficacy of the criteria. Later, he recounts principles for solving disagreements at work as:

1. "Put our honest thoughts out on the table,
2. Have thoughtful disagreements in which people are willing to shift their opinions as they learn, and
3. Have agreed-upon ways of deciding (e.g. voting, having clear authorities) if disagreements remain so that we can move beyond them without resentments."[101]

Thus, I would like to propose some suggestions and questions to be considered in order to drive a collection of principles. These are principles I want to adhere to, have a ring of truth in them to me, and what I desire to be known for, as well.

ARTICULATING YOUR PRINCIPLES

What are your guiding principles? Are these two ideas distinct? Or do you see them as the same—moral ideals that you want to be truth for you? If you had to articulate three-to-five principles or values you would not intentionally compromise with your decisions or actions, what would they be?

For me, I articulate these as

---

[101] Ray Dalio, *Principles: Life and Work*.

1. Be honest and seek truth: act honestly, and be a truth-teller and truth-seeker
2. Be generous: give of your resources—time, thought, and money
3. Be excellent: anything worth doing is worth doing well, and excellence takes passion which means suffering
4. Give grace: meet myself and others where they are

These four principles ring true to how I act, intend to act, and I believe other people would say my life reflects these most of the time.

My fourth principle, give grace, is of critical importance to me. There are days and times when something or everything goes wrong, or when we have a lapse in judgment. We make a mistake. We act outside of our principles. Does this mean we are hypocrites? Does this mean our principles are no longer our truth? I would argue no.

In the same way, someone might give a poor presentation one day, but it does not mean their reputation and credibility in giving presentations is destroyed permanently, especially if there was a body of work that built the reputation and credibility in the first place. It's like running a marathon: practiced effort day by day. Being thoughtful, engaging in reflection, keeping a journal, and seeking feedback are all ways to think through one's truth and gauge the effect of any uncharacteristic behavior.

ADHERING TO YOUR PRINCIPLES

I once had the great pleasure of attending a conference focused on ethics. I had been tangentially involved in the marketing of the conference and knew that its speakers were largely Christian. What I didn't expect was to hear so many stories from down-to-earth, well-educated, and incredibly inspiring and ambitious business leaders who gave the credit for many high points in their careers to God.

For example, one man who gave a short talk about his career and how his faith related to his work gave a simple yet profound example of a short interaction. As a prominent leader and co-founder at a private equity firm, he walks into the office one day and sees a woman waiting, seated in the lobby. She looks somewhat apprehensive and, knowing it is unlikely that she knows his role at the firm, he takes a seat nearby and asks what she is doing there today. She was interviewing for a role at the firm, he learned, so he asked, "why do you want to work here?" She, with a resolute look on her face, said, "While it might not be true in all cases, in my case, this is the only company that I've interacted with in this industry that I would feel fully comfortable as a woman working here—without the concern of being hit on or asked for more."

When the speaker told this story, the reality that this is probably commonplace was realized by many in the room. Most of us knew, and some who worked in certain related industries before business school had personally experienced, what the woman alluded to.

A different speaker during the conference recounted his role in finance and a story with colleagues after leaving the office. He explained that it was common for a group of colleagues from his work to grab dinner or drinks after work together—whether to blow off steam, unwind from the day, or build camaraderie. This day, with some drinks in the group, someone suggested they go to a strip club.

Nervously, he walked along with the group, thinking about what he could do. He could go in, not make a big deal of it, and just be with the others. But what would he tell his wife? Or would he tell her? Or he could not go. Would he be fired? Or eventually nudged out for not being part of the culture? Or would he walk away from the job himself? This last option came to fruition, as he went home and told his wife that he would have to find another job. And she respected him all the more for his decision.

In both cases, these men acted according to their values, some guiding principles that helped them either build safe company culture or think through decisions. In one case, he founded and built a company where women were valued for professional contributions and promoted a safe culture for women. This culture, he recounted, was attributed to his faith, how we are to treat others with dignity and respect and always treat them as having inherent value in God's eyes. In the other case, he walked away from a job so as not to compromise his values for himself and with his wife in marriage.

We all will be challenged at some point with ethical issues. These two stories show hope for being principled. I believe it helps to reflect on ethical issues and articulate one's principles, perhaps even write them down. At the end of the day, what do we want to stand for? We may fall short, but having principles provides guideposts for navigating uncertainty, change, and the unexpected.

SPEAK ABOUT THAT WHICH IS UNSPOKEN

I feel so strongly about truth-telling and seeking truth that I want to highlight one example. My hope is not necessarily that you will adopt the principle of honesty but rather that you will be encouraged to be honest with yourself about your own values and ethics. That we might all ask the hard questions of ourselves and others, because I think this concept ties with critical importance to the concept of vision and purpose or the mantra, *"embrace change—experiment often—learn humbly."*

During one of my classes, an author and leader at a prominent home appliances company was a guest speaker. She presented the framework that she developed in her book. After she spoke, a line of people formed to get their book copy signed.

During the next class, my professor asked whether the class noticed anything about who comprised the line—everyone in the line was a woman. Why did no men want to get their book signed? Could it be that women have an easier time connecting with men's stories, but maybe not vice versa? Regardless, the professor recounted asking another professor if he should even bring this up; that professor said, "I would never raise that in class," to which my professor asked: "why?" She received the response: "Because you don't know where it's going to go." My professor asked our class the question the next week.

Sometimes, not knowing where something will go means you've found an important question to ask. Our society should do this more. We should do this more with our peers, colleagues, clients, customers, adversaries, and family. Imagine the dialogue and conversations we could have. Emergence can sometimes only happen if given the opportunity—open the door, ask the question, conduct the experiment. If you don't, you'll never know.

PRACTICING PRINCIPLES

In congruence with the major theme of this book, I would encourage readers to think through their values and principles. What behavior does one truly want to be known for? What does someone care to measure him or herself against? And importantly, these can change over time and are not intended to be "attained" or "strived for" like a vision or a purpose. In some ways, they should already ring true and be a natural part of one's character. What's important is to open our eyes and hearts to think about them, acknowledge them, and use them as a positive tool for navigating life. They might just create a loving marriage, attract customers, and most importantly, lead others.

CHAPTER 11

CONCLUSION

The beauty of it is that it could fail.
—PROFESSOR HARRY DAVIS

At the beginning of this book, while recounting the story of the boy lost in the desert searching for treasure and his personal legend, I invited you to explore a series of questions as I recounted a handful of stories of people who have navigated uncertainty. They were:

- How do expert "navigators of life" think? How do successful, "emergent" lives come about?
- What skills can you build to position you for anything? How can you build them?
- How do you grow your potential and capabilities in all directions?
- What questions should you be asking yourself, and when?
- Who do you surround yourself with along the way?
- What about when life happens? Can you stay emergent and curious?
- What are the lies you tell yourself?

In chapter six, after recounting a variety of stories of people who have navigated uncertainty, I provided ways to *embrace change, experiment often, learn humbly* based on learnings from the stories. While these takeaways do not provide exhaustive answers to the questions posed, I hope they serve as quick reference points to prompt thought.

1. Don't believe the lies you tell yourself
2. Just keep moving
3. Stay curious
4. Treat life as art, not science
5. "Expect the tiger to be tricky"[102]
6. Make allies
7. Process experiences
8. Set the intention, not the outcome
9. Know thyself
10. Be relentless

In subsequent chapters, we reviewed several frameworks and actions anyone can take with a group or as an individual to spur reflection, exploration, experimentation, and learning.

FRAMEWORKS:
- Robert Knapp's "Sprint"
- Ed Catmull and Pixar's "Braintrust"
- Ed Catmull and Pixar's "Postmortem"
- Harry Davis's "Existential strategy: Just keep moving"

---

[102] Ed Catmull and Amy Wallace, *Creativity Inc.: Overcoming the Unseen Forces That Stand in the Way of True Inspiration*, chap. 7.

- Robert Quinn's "Fundamental State of Leadership"
- Harry Davis's "Stage Page + Complete Strategist"
- Rebecca Beagan's "Experiment Experience"

"ANYTIME" RESET TACTICS:
- Take a retreat with an intention
- Take a Shultz hour
- Talk to humans
- Give a "lollipop"
- Be your own "Runway Harry"
- Dream it up in a world of impossibility

All these drive toward the overarching message: *embrace change, experiment often, learn humbly.*

With the overview above of the key content in this book, I want to begin closing by inviting some visualization on what we're trying to do here.

Ed Catmull from Pixar says it well in *Creativity, Inc.*:

"In A Bug's Life, Bob says, Andrew compared making a movie to an archaeological dig. This adds yet another element to the picture - the idea that as you progress, your project is revealing itself to you. 'You're digging away, and you don't know what dinosaur you're digging for,' Bob says. 'Then, you reveal a little bit of it. And you may be digging in two different places at once and you think what you have is one thing, but as you go farther and farther, blindly digging, it starts revealing itself. Once you start getting a glimpse of it, you know how better to dig.' Bob and Andrew have heard me voice my objection to this particular *metaphor many times. As I've said, I believe that when we work on a movie, we are not uncovering an existing thing that had the bad luck to get buried under eons of sediment; we are creating something new. But they argue that the idea of the movie is in there somewhere - think of David, trapped in Michelangelo's block of marble - helps them stay on track and not lose hope. So while I started this chapter by insisting that what moviegoers see on the screen does not emerge fully formed from some visionary's brain, I have to allow for this idea: Having faith that the elements of the movie are all there for us to find often sustains us during the search...just recognize that...not every bone you unearth will necessarily belong to the skeleton you are trying to assemble."*[103]

Whether you agree with Andrew and Bob or with Ed, I don't think it matters. Whether you believe one discovers their purpose in life that was waiting to be revealed or whether one believes that purpose, in a sense, is crafted through a series of choices (that life is composed like a piece of music through experiments and experiences), what I care most about is the understanding that forward movement with either philosophy takes paying attention, consideration, effort, and decisions.

More concretely, through this book, I hope to have relayed some interesting stories and identified patterns for how some highly successful people are expert navigators of life. They try many different things, they are able to "just go with it," and they embrace change. It is so important and powerful to be open to emergence, so that I do not prescribe my life before

---

103 Harry Davis, "Creativity," session seven.

living it, but rather write my story every day. But make no mistake, it does take *writing*.

I never considered myself an exceptional writer, but I'm writing this book. Katharine Graham was not a manager, but she managed and led. Lou Gerstner was not a technology guy, but he turned around one of the biggest technology companies of our time. Michelle Obama was not the "Princeton type" in the eyes of her primary-school teachers, but she graduated from Princeton and went on to Harvard Law School. Professor Harry Davis is also Runway Harry. Elephants can't dance—until *they do*.

What can you write, manage, turn around, earn, and become? Don't worry so much about what's on the paper but put something down. And put "draft" on everything. I think that teams and corporations can adopt a similar mindset for innovation and change, as well, staying nimble to emerging trends, market dynamics, and technological change, for example, by investing in experiments to build value in gaining insights for whether and how to move forward. A partner at the management consulting firm for which I work *does* put "draft" on everything as a symbol to our clients of the importance of staying nimble to the dynamics of a changing world and the quality of our thought as learning happens.

And when you can't or don't want *to do* anything, that's okay. Know that while I have relayed stories of pushing boundaries, rejecting lies, and experimenting through life, this book is also about finding your voice. That our lives are not dependent on accomplishing a vision or purpose, as a well-crafted vision statement is not about the attainment of a finite end, but rather the impact by a continued pursuit—i.e. not dictated by *what we do*, but rather by *who we are* and the guiding principles we adopt or succumb to as a part of who we are.

Coming full circle with the start of this book, I explained that a partner at my company requested that I read *The Alchemist*. If you recall, I assumed it had to do with chemicals because we were starting a chemical industry project. In *The Alchemist*, there is a small portion of the book where alchemy is present, where lead is turned into gold. This is like a metaphor for our lives.

We go through experiences that shape us, change us, really, and the beauty is that they add texture to our lives. And through the guideposts above, I would only encourage us to take Santiago's example of being at peace with doubt in our lives. Do whatever you're doing now to the best of your ability. Follow the signs to the next step, as Santiago did. Seek the lesson and learning in everything. By doing so, I think we set ourselves up for a life where "Embrace change, experiment often, learn Humbly" comes to us more simply as an integrated part of our behavior, mindset, and lives.

I want to close this chapter with some words from a primary source of inspiration for this book, Ed Catmull:

"I often say that managers of creative enterprises must hold lightly to goals and firmly to intentions. What does that mean? It means that we must be open to having our goals change as we learn new information or are surprised by things we thought we knew but didn't. As long as our

intentions—our value—remain constant, our goals can shift as needed. At Pixar, we try never to waver in our ethics, our values, and our intention to create original, quality products. We are willing to adjust our goals as we learn, striving to get it right—not necessarily to get it right the first time. Because that, to my mind, is the only way to establish something else that is essential to creativity: a culture that protects the new."[104]

In the next and final chapter, I want to tell one last story—my own.

---

[104] Ed Catmull and Amy Wallace, *Creativity Inc.: Overcoming the Unseen Forces That Stand in the Way of True Inspiration*, chap. 7.

CHAPTER 12

MY STORY OF CHANGE

What makes you vulnerable makes you beautiful.
—BRENÉ BROWN

While I feel I have covered the content—the stories, frameworks, and practices—that I wished to cover, when the idea for what I wanted to write about emerged, for anyone curious about my recent personal story on emergence, experimentation, and learning, I invite you to read a section from a paper that I submitted to Professor Harry Davis on March 20, 2019.

The below excerpt was for our final paper submission for Professor Davis's Business Policy class. His class played a significant role, as I'm sure you can tell from the stories and frameworks I have provided, in the framing of this book. I tell the story of how I went form "not being a runner" to running a marathon, conquering forever the lie I have told myself since throwing up in the hallway of my elementary school after trying to run a mile, a lie about what I could do, who I was, and where I could go: "I am not a runner."

REDACTED EXCERPT FROM FINAL PAPER FOR HARRY DAVIS'S BUSINESS POLICY COURSE, MARCH 2019:
In September 2017, Chicago Booth's Stacey Kole presented a provocation to the Class of 2019. "Write down why you are here. Right now, jot down why you are beneath this roof Harper today. What brought you here? What do you hope to accomplish? Now, don't forget it." That day, like a bright-eyed, bushy-tailed incoming MBA candidate, I pulled out my computer and wrote an electronic post-it on my laptop's desktop:

My goals at Booth:

- Deepen knowledge (academics high priority)
- Attend speaker events
- Add an income stream
- Create my app for matching needs/service
- Know what theme I want to bring to the world when I graduate.

From time to time, whether bidding for courses or deciding whether to attend an event or social gathering, I would vaguely think about this post-it and its implications on my underlying priorities. I would go on to take the Application Development course to create the app I mentioned on the post-it. I would take rigorous courses to truly challenge my biases and methodological frames and to build new skillsets, like Data-Driven Marketing, Financial Statement Analysis, Strategy Lab, and Pricing Strategies.

Yet I would struggle with defining a book topic for a book-writing program I had become involved with and writing a purpose statement for a non-Booth Christian mentorship program called Emerging Leadership Initiative (ELI) of which I'm a part. These post-it goals showed an inner desire to learn, gaining exposure to new content in various forms, and to apply, even if I didn't know how. Booth was my stage for the next twenty months. So, it was time to step out from behind the curtain.

* * *

My MBA started out shaky. By a few weeks in, I wondered if I had made a grave mistake. I was incredibly insecure about my social belonging—who were my friends? What did people think about me? Why hadn't I been invited to that brunch? To make matters worse, the first bullet on my post-it note for why I was at Booth was in question. Was I deepening my knowledge?

I was taking four courses, the three foundations, including one advanced version, and a fourth class in entrepreneurship. Yet I felt that I wasn't learning as much from the foundational courses that were similar to my undergraduate business courses, albeit with more reading to do. I was spending endless hours at night and on weekends reading the assigned course material, all while saying no to social gatherings to try to accomplish this deepening of knowledge goal. I had taken the foundations courses as a BBA at Michigan Ross, and while some of the content was more advanced, I knew, inevitably, that the most incremental content would likely be forgotten over time, as it was incredibly theoretical.

More important than all of this, though, I experienced a sort of culture shock in my faith life. I had been faithfully attending a church in Michigan every week and attended a weekly small group. I was surrounded by people who wanted to serve others, and volunteering in some capacity in the community or in the church congregation was the norm.

In contrast, at Booth, "me," "myself," and "I" was the spoken language, which I logically understood due to the investment of time and money that people were making. I was not a career-switcher, as I was being sponsored by the management consulting firm for which I had worked for four years before Booth. So, I fortunately did not have the same pressure as my peers. But still, it was all different.

So, I did what I am prone to do as a "feeler," according to the Myers-Briggs Type Indicator. I cried. I was stuck. My first quarter was mediocre. I didn't have the depth of friendships I had hoped for. And I felt like I couldn't be myself.

* * *

Through a re-grounding with my family and my faith at the holidays, I returned to Booth in January 2018 with a renewed sense of fortitude. First and foremost, I picked my church and attended every week, being renewed by the Gospel and power of Christ each week. And everything flowed over time from there. Grace for others and their ambitions to progress their careers and grace for myself and my transition into a new city and environment.

Winter quarter turned around and was good. But spring quarter was even better. I had met a fellow first-year student named Leon during spring break whom I hadn't met before.

After landing in Bogota, Colombia for a 350-person trip with my graduate school classmates, I saw him.

I was intrigued, so I went up to him and asked, without introducing myself: "Do you dance?"

He looked at me with a questioning look in his dark brown eyes: "Uh, yeah."

"We're going to dance together on this trip," I replied, and I walked away. We went on to dance together almost every evening in Bogota, Medellin, and Cartagena.

Leon and I hit it off. I craved to learn his thoughts on every subject, to know his favorite song and share mine, to be spontaneous again (something that is true to my character but had been shut down in adult life, similarly to Santiago's childhood dreams). Deeper friendships with ladies at Booth also blossomed with the spring flowers. And all was well.

* * *

Summer flew by and fall quarter crisply started. There were ups and downs along the way, but there was movement. There were experiments, like fostering a puppy. I had grown up with pets but hadn't had one of my own. I knew once I started back in management consulting, I would not be able to have a pet with the travel schedule, so I fostered three sweet puppies during my second year at Booth.

There were fun times, like returning to my alma mater, the University of Michigan, for a November football game with

Leon shortly after he officially became my boyfriend. But deep down, there was still a stirring. A subconscious countdown to June 15, 2019—graduation day.

Would I come out of my MBA with my post-it accomplished: deeper knowledge, speaker events attended, an income stream added, an app created, and knowing what theme I wanted to bring to the world? Or had my goals changed?

Accomplishing the specific goals on the post-it became less important as I realized that checkmarks can still leave an unsettled feeling. The last goal, knowing what theme I wanted to bring to the world, was the closest to capturing what might give a settled feeling, or at least a content one, on June 15, 2019. The underlying and stirring strategic questions I was subconsciously asking myself were: what theme do you bring to the world, Rebecca? What characters are on your stage page? Moreover, what is your personal leadership philosophy?

* * *

On a return flight from Australia on January 6, 2019, at the end of the holiday break between quarters, I brainstormed my experiments for first quarter of 2019, part of an experiment/goal-setting practice that I had started about six months earlier. During the course of our Australia trip after Christmas, we had read *Becoming* by Michelle Obama together; he had read a couple of other books; and I had read Lou Gerstner's *Who Says Elephants Can't Dance*.

We felt inspired. And reflective. So, I developed more goals than usual in Quarter 1 of 2019. Some included: progress to

Phase 2 in Chicago Booth's New Venture Challenge, participate in the Alumni New Venture Challenge at Booth, run a marathon, take more dance classes, participate in the Believers in Business faith-based case competition, and pray more. These and the foray of other goals I wrote down were in addition to previously committing to being a co-chair of two Booth Groups, facilitating a Booth Insights small group throughout the quarter, and participating in a non-Booth Christian mentorship program each week.

Within a day of landing in Chicago from Australia in early January, I was setting out to accomplish the goals that I had established. Soon it became evident that doing everything would be impossible. Quality was going to be at the expense of quantity unless something changed. And I didn't get the balance quite right, as admittedly quality suffered in some areas of commitment. Nevertheless, I prioritized marathon training over dancing more, over the amount of yoga I would have liked to have practiced, and over some social gatherings. If you miss a long run in marathon training, it can put your entire training at risk. Luckily, the friends and loved ones in my life—my treasured support network—understood and gave nothing but encouragement in my endeavor to run a marathon.

* * *

Two weeks into marathon training, however, I hit my first crucible—my hamstrings were on fire and I was worried that I had pulled a muscle. The difficulty with training is that, if you skip a run, long or short, even for one day, you can be set back. So I had to decide whether to run again the next day, when my hamstrings were still overly sore, or rest. I rested. To me, this was a decision about the long-game, because an injury could mean not even being able to start the race on race day. This was the first of a few physical qualms during training.

Within weeks of each other, I would find out whether the NVC team I had joined would progress to Phase 2 and would run the marathon.

And, I failed.

The team that I had joined did not advance to Phase 2 of Booth's New Venture Challenge. But, days before, we learned we had been accepted into Harvard's final round of pitches for its Real Estate Conference. Though we did not win the HBS pitch competition, I had the great opportunity to witness nine other teams from top schools around the United States and Canada, and was able to catalog my learnings to feed into the ANVC team I am on. Though the outcome was not what I had hoped for, I gained a different opportunity nonetheless.

Then came marathon weekend. In a similar way to how George Shultz, former Secretary of State to President Ronald Reagan, using gardening to illustrate the importance of tending to something over time to see results, running a marathon is the same. You commit to the effort and train your body over time. My training happened to run in parallel with the assignment to read Katharine Graham's *Personal History*.

Like a meet-cute, my training and Katharine Graham's journey collided and took me to new ideas. I listened to the self-narrated audiobook of Katharine Graham's book while I trained. Since it was so cold outside in Chicago, I was bound to the treadmill, but in some ways, it worked out for the best. I would listen to Katharine's light-hearted voice while in a running portion, then would write down my thoughts during a walking portion of my training. Katharine Graham became my running lullaby, her crucibles became my balm. And training continued.

* * *

It was race weekend. I had been waiting to write this part of this paper because marathon weekend was March 15-18, 2019, the weekend before the paper's due date. But I knew that the marathon was important to this story. Katharine Graham had emerged as my lullaby during marathon training. I wanted to provide the space and opportunity for insight and learning to emerge from the marathon. And I also had an intuition that the marathon would be a breakthrough and/or a test of my action skills, translating knowledge and/or thinking into action.

Leon (who was training all along with me for the marathon, which would be his sixth marathon) and I were running late to the airport on Friday evening, March 15, in rush-hour traffic, but we made our flight. We arrived to Asheville, NC hungry and tired. We loaded up on carbs at a local Italian restaurant that was luckily open at 9:45 p.m. The next day was the race expo, where we picked up our runner's bibs, swag, and goodies. But we also got to see maps of the elevation and hills, revisit the time cut-offs, and with each new piece of information, my confidence waned.

What if I couldn't do it? What if the hours and hours and hours that I had put into training for this marathon had been for naught? What would Leon think of me? What would my friends think of me, who had decorated my door with encouragement and protein- and electrolyte-packed snacks? I was experiencing the doubt that I had written about in my first individual paper for Business Policy, the unexpected trait that can be a positive, overlooked leadership behavior. Similarly to what I wrote about, I was experiencing doubt like Santiago from *The Alchemist* experienced in his journey.

Then, it was race morning—I hadn't slept well at all. Then, the scheduled Uber had cancelled so we were waiting for a late ride, yet we entered the gates one minute before runners were required to be on the property. My nerves were on end, perhaps because of the thirty-five-degree temperatures. Then, it was 7:30 a.m., Sunday morning, and I pressed start on my Apple watch's outdoor run feature.

To my delight, I was running. I was doing it. I decided not to turn on my wireless headphones in my ears that would connect to my mobile phone and play the sermons and music I had downloaded the night before. I just wanted to focus on my breathing. And to my surprise, I was able to regulate my breathing and catch a pace.

My grief and fear about the higher elevation air, the cold temperatures, my hip that had been hurting, the swelling blisters on my feet—not to mention the fact that some people had been training for eleven months while I had been training for nine—weeks, were being confronted with flashbacks from my life.

I remembered that in fifth grade, my class was required to "run a mile," and I was one of the last to finish. I subsequently downed a bottle of water and shortly thereafter threw it up.

I remembered in sixth grade how I could never keep up on the gym class runs.

I remembered how in about ninth grade, my best friend Tiffany and I were outside trying to jog. She said, "Beck, just get to the next grass blade, get to the next gravel."

I remembered my parents in those strides, their struggles, and my dad's successful battle with cancer.

Countless memories and flashbacks from my life came to mind. And the pressing question came to mind: why are you running, Rebecca? And unprovoked, I felt the pressure of tears behind my eyes as I ran. I realized that I ran because I had always told myself that I couldn't. Yet, deep down, I knew that I could.

And there was beauty in the possibility of failure. There always is, because it is an opportunity to confront your character. And to see, with time, what you do next. In the end, it is not about succeeding or failing, but about the journey, and whether it was one you are proud of and content with.

I had set a vision and then followed through with putting in the work and doing the minutes-per-mile math needed to hit the checkpoints. I had planned the journey well and knew what I needed to do. The cut-off was 6.5 hours. I had written on a piece of paper the night before the cut-off times at miles six, 7.5, ten, 12.5, and seventeen miles and stuffed it in my pocket, even though the times were forged into my memory.

So I just kept moving, adopting the existential strategy that Harry Davis taught in his course at Booth and that Lou Gerstner adopted when he turned around IBM. I oscillated between jogging and walking to save my knees for the long-haul. I was probably under-conditioned due to only training for nine weeks, but I was going for finishing my first marathon.

Of course, the miles kept dragging on and on. The hills became infinitely more strenuous to traverse. And my knees were really feeling it. Yet, somehow, I had prepared, and my pace was still good. I had hit all of the cut-off checkpoints early and was in the home stretch after mile seventeen. Of course, I had been warned. Like the last few miles of hiking the Grand Canyon, which Leon and I had done last Memorial Day, this stretch was the hardest.

* * *

A little over a year earlier, I had hiked the Grand Canyon with Leon, and part of what pushed me through was the existential strategy: when there is no other option, just keep moving. During the marathon running, I repeated this to myself multiple times. And I remembered to take the water, Gatorade, and electrolyte and nutrition gel shots provided every few miles to satisfy near-term needs, giving my body the necessary provisions for the journey.

Since learning about the existential strategy, I have embraced it as a part of my personal mantra, unashamedly. While other manifestations of strategy are powerful and inspiring, "just keep moving" has been unexpectedly but delightfully impactful to me because, like Santiago's doubt, I think it is an overlooked, but incredibly powerful strategy.

Like Lou Gerstner's approach with IBM, sometimes, you need to just keep moving, despite the constant pressure from the world to set a vision. I have adapted it somewhat for how I try to approach others. For me, this idea has also become meet people where they are. Perhaps people have no set vision, or no real options. Meet them there, in their circumstances. This has allowed me to incorporate my personal faith, as well—give grace to others and self. Take a dynamic view, not a static view of the world.

* * *

At 1:30 p.m. EST on March 17, 2019, I completed my first marathon. Not knowing whether I would burst into tears or collapse on the ground upon crossing the finish line, I braced for anything. And what came was calm.

But wait. Running the 26.2 mile marathon is over. Life goes on. Now what? I submit my final projects and papers for winter quarter and set off on a flight to Southeast Asia. How similar it seems to a few months earlier, setting off on a flight to Australia. And a few months before that, setting off on a flight to Europe. But that's life. That's every day. We wake up, set about our day's journey, and end up somewhere at the end of the day. Sometimes, all things went as expected throughout our day, sometimes not. Sometimes tragedy strikes, sometimes we strike gold. But two things are consistent: 1) not knowing for sure where we will end up and 2) deciding how we start each day. What I've gained is a lens on how to start my day.

At different points in life, we have decisions to make, but these decisions cannot be fully planned for, because the circumstances in which we live are constantly changing. While having a vision and goals for one's life can provide general direction and prioritization around decisions, they should not be so rigid as to place barriers against possibility.

What I have found in these last few months through my involvement in Emerging Leaders Initiative mentorship program, my MBA courses, and Creators Book Program is that purpose is bespoke according to the circumstances we're in, the (perhaps unexpected) people we meet, our health, and more. Purpose can be written and re-written. For me, principles and core values are what drive more consistency, as they resonate more with a static state of my character—honesty, generosity, and excellence.

From grade school to the present, countless examples of these three core values come to mind. Yet my "purpose" is not so well-defined. Some might say it is because I haven't discovered it yet. However, I would say that the answer is more akin to Maya Angelou's wisdom: "I've learned that people will forget what you said, people will forget what you did, but people will never forget how you made them feel." For me, this resonates as being consistent in living out and having a legacy in my underlying core value and guiding principles versus some resounding and profound achievement I want to attain.

I desire to live honestly, generously, and with excellence, to the glory of my God, giving grace to others and self. Perhaps this is my purpose, even if not as specific as leadership trainings try to extract. Perhaps purpose is about a way of being, dynamic, not static. Living in a strategy space where discovery is celebrated rather than a maintenance space where execution is celebrated. Remembering that I am the playwright and the director and can reset the stage as depths of the actors and characters—i.e. the circumstances and the people—change.

* * *

Circling back to that day when Stacey Kole, deputy dean for MBA Programs, encouraged us to think through why were at Booth. I think her question was spot-on. I did not fully understand my own answer—to learn and to apply—until almost five-sixths of the way through the journey. And I missed some things on that post-it—how profoundly important my friendships and relationships would be. And I never anticipated gaining a love like I've never experienced before. One endeavor (participating in New Venture Challenge) failed, another (running a 26.2 mile marathon) conquered.

So what does it all mean? Upon reflection, and perhaps on runner's high somewhere in my second hour of the marathon, I laid tapestry in my head for my personal philosophy, my leadership framework—my playbook—if you will.

On the same trip in Australia, when so many dreams started forming and plans were made, I asked Leon a question while we were driving along the Great Ocean Road outside of Melbourne: "Do you have a personal leadership mantra or philosophy? What might it be?" To which he reciprocated the question and I said something along the lines of "Be inspiring yet tough, and consistently reasonable," which fell flat when he heard me say it. What I didn't know then is what I am perhaps only beginning to discover now, something that I will keep getting to know throughout the years I am given. Something that hours of running, jogging, walking, and the flashings of my life, my failures, my internally-driven put-downs, and my externally-driven condescension, sparked learning in me.

My life is unwritten. And that's okay. People will ask for a purpose. And I will give them a draft and my principles, with an asterisk for "*subject to change." I wasn't a runner. And yet, I ran. And ran. So for me, goals have now become experiments. What experiment will I undertake next?

The framing is completely different for me—rather than a heavy approach of pure discipline, I now have a lighter mindset of curiosity, openness, and exploration, recognizing it is good to think about things one wants to endeavor, but that change is almost inevitable. And that is the beauty of the experiment. To experiment, to reflect, to learn, to repeat.

After reflecting on the fact that I am not advancing with the team I had joined to Phase 2 of New Venture Challenge, I realized that I have an opportunity. I can experiment with something else should I choose. And I think that I will—because ultimately, New Venture Challenge wasn't a goal in and of itself. For me, it was about exploring entrepreneurship, as it has long been something I've dreamed about, since childhood. So, an experiment that I am incredibly excited about for spring quarter 2019 is trying and testing one of the thirty-four business ideas I have come up with the last few years.

I learned perhaps life's most simple and commonsense lesson at Booth. Our life is emergent. Our life is unwritten. Our life stumbles forward sometimes. Nevertheless, let us emerge. Let us take up the pen and write. Let us stumble. For, like the beauty of creativity is that it could fail, the beauty in life is living it, emerging from the planned and the unplanned, and repeating. As Walt Whitman writes and Professor Keating quotes in *Dead Poets Society*:

"Oh Me! Oh Life!" - By Walt Whitman

Oh me! Oh life! of the questions of these recurring,
Of the endless trains of the faithless, of cities fill'd
with the foolish,
Of myself forever reproaching myself, (for who
more foolish than I, and who more faithless?)
Of eyes that vainly crave the light, of the objects
mean, of the struggle ever renew'd,
Of the poor results of all, of the plodding and sor-
did crowds I see around me,
Of the empty and useless years of the rest, with the
rest me intertwined,
The question, O me! so sad, recurring—What good
amid these, O me, O life?
Answer.
That you are here—that life exists and identity,
That the powerful play goes on, and you may con-
tribute a verse.

In *Dead Poets Society*, Professor Keating follows with: "What will your verse be?"

So, I will soon submit this paper to Professor Davis and soon board my flight to Southeast Asia with Leon, my boyfriend and fellow Boothie. This time, we both packed blank journals—for we foresee some Shultz hours, perhaps by Angkor Wat temples in Cambodia, perhaps on the beaches of El Nido in the Philippines. And I cannot wait for the thinking, exploration, experimentation, dialogue, dreaming, goal-setting, verse-writing, and subsequent failing and succeeding that is to come. I cannot wait to build upon the learnings from winter quarter 2019 of my MBA, writing the manuscript of my book, currently titled "Draft."

* * *

Writing the final paper for my course at Booth and writing this book provided space for reflection on the goal I had set for myself when I started at Booth: *know what theme I want to bring to the world when I graduate*. I realized that I have not failed in this goal but, at the same time, I do not have a one-word, final answer. Rather, I know that I want to bring the themes of embracing change, experimentation, and learning. These three themes enable me to overcome the lies I have told myself while meeting others where they are. I hope that readers might consider these themes, as well as the ten takeaways, and through reflection think of the themes and principles for one's own life.

Finally, I ask you to reflect on something. Reflect on the root definition of "passion." It is commonly misunderstood in today's times to mean desire or object of one's enthusiasm. And when a person is confronted throughout life with the questions I started with . . .

- "What do you want to be when you grow up?"
- "What is your purpose?"
- "What is your vision for your career?"

... often one thinks about where one's passion lies.

But, the word "passion" comes from the Latin root pati-, meaning suffering or enduring.[105] Perhaps this is even more appropriate in understanding how to think about the questions above. The definition prompts us to think about what we are willing to suffer for, not in a painful sense necessarily, but in an enduring sense. And I think my themes provide a way to manage and navigate this passion or suffering, knowing that uncertainty may come, experimenting may help maintain nimbleness, and learning guides the next step.

For me, learning the definition of "passion" brought new light to the film *The Passion of the Christ* or *The 'Suffering' of the Christ*. I know that Christ suffered for me because of His love. I am worth it to him. I will never forget this, and His love and example guide my purpose and my principles. No amount of achievement or attainment of a title, a position, or a salary will bring "the good life." Rather, the good life is being united with Christ.

In my own day-to-day, I am also empowered to ask myself,: *why did I run the Asheville Marathon on March 17?* Was it because I had a strong desire or enthusiasm? Did I do it for Leon? Or is it because I saw value in the suffering, the enduring? I saw value in taking one step, and then

---

[105] "Passion."

another. Yes, in life there is the possibility of failure, especially for things that are worth suffering for. But there is the inevitability of learning if open to discovery. I will try never to forget this lesson. On March 22, 2020, I will hit the pavement once again, a half-marathon this time. And I look forward to writing verses, step after step, mile after mile, asking myself: *what are you experimenting with these days?*

* * *

> "*When I fall, I shall rise; when I sit in darkness, the Lord will be a light to me.*"
> MICAH 7:8 ESV

ACKNOWLEDGMENTS

I have to start by thanking my parents, Mary and Bob, and my sister, Rachel. You shaped me, you raised me, and you encouraged me to dream.

Thanks to Leon for inspiring many of the stories and the topic of this book. You were my hiking partner in the Grand Canyon, my adventure partner in Australia, my dancing partner in Colombia, and more. Looking forward to the journey ahead.

Special thanks to Stephanie Wisner for inviting me into the book writing program cohort at the University of Chicago and for her partnership and encouragement throughout the book writing process. Looking forward to reading your book!

Thanks to Eric Koester, founder of Creator Institute. Without your coaching, this book would not have been written. Thank you for never giving up on me and encouraging me to write my verse, becoming a writer.

Thanks to everyone from the New Degree Press team who helped me so much. Special thanks to Brian, head of publishing, Linda, my manuscript editor, Gina, my copy editor, and Dania, my cover designer.

Finally, thanks to the staff at Blue Stripes Cacao Shop in New York City. Much of this book was written in this vibrant shop on 13th Street while sipping coffee and nibbling on delectable cacao treats.

With special thanks to the many supporters who made publishing possible through your generous contributions:

David Anderson, Mary and Robert Beagan, Amelia and Luc Berger, Yarden Berkman, Brandon and Heather Boyle, Melanie Brown, Danny and Valerie Burnside, Lynette Carlson, Rebecca Centanni, Arthur Chow and Leeda Wang, Blake Davis, Brandon Douglass, Jane Dutton, Olufunbi Eboda, Ashley Edwards, Leon Evans, Brian Gersh, Jasper Goldberg and Elise Hogan, John Hand, Gareth Hayes, Sarah and Tom Hefty, Paul Howes, Carolyn and David Jackson, Mallika Kantamneni, Joseph and Marcia Kennedy, Jina Kim, Margie King, Bradley Kirchoff, Rachel and Ken Kirchoff, Eloise Kirchoff, Eric Koester, Olivia Korostelina, Aniket Kumar, Ashley Lee, Barbara-Maria Loth, Zeeshan Mahmood, Chris Martinovich, Leah and Alex McIntosh, Michael Murphy, Shahid Murtuza, Patrick O'Brien, Kallie Parchman, Alexander Porzondek, Maria Ptouchkina, Mathieu Rasamoela, Anne Reilly, Delano Saporu, Douglas Sexauer, Sonal Somaiya, Sarah Spitery, Gretchen Spreitzer, Patrick Street, Daniel Tao, Kavya Thota, Brittany Vanderbeek, Kyle Veatch, Kenneth and Peggy Voigt, Marybeth Voigt, Chris White, Joseph Wiles, Dana Wilson, Stephanie Wisner, Maureen Wu, Kelsey Zehentbauer, Samantha Zeluck, Annabelle Zhang

RESOURCES

FOR MORE ON BRAINTRUSTS, VISIT:
https://medium.com/great-business-stories/lessons-from-pixar-1-the-braintrust-e306843a5153

https://www.fastcompany.com/3027135/inside-the-pixar-braintrust

FOR MORE ON POST MORTEMS, VISIT:
https://www.skmurphy.com/blog/2007/02/01/pixars-ed-catmull-highlights-value-of-post-mortems/

physicianleaders.org/news/take-morbidity-and-mortality-reviews-to-infinity-and-beyond

FOR MORE ON THE FUNDAMENTAL STATE OF LEADERSHIP, TAKE A LOOK HERE:
https://hbr.org/2005/07/moments-of-greatness-entering-the-fundamental-state-of-leadership

https://positiveorgs.bus.umich.edu/articles/entering-the-fundamental-state-of-leadership-a-framework-for-the-positive-transformation-of-self-and-others/

FOR MORE ON THE STAGE PAGE TOOL, GO HERE:
http://morassociates.com/2009conf/2009conffiles/Davis-ITLP-Conf-2009.pdf

http://www.morassociates.com/2008conf/HarryDavisITLeadershippdf.pdf

RESOURCE FOR LOLLIPOP MOMENTS:
https://pharmacademy.org/system/files/lollipop_moments_in_leadership_final_0.pdf

https://www.drewdudley.com/

APPENDIX

CHAPTER 1
"Alchemy." Lexico, Powered by Oxford.
https://www.lexico.com/en/definition/alchemy.

Coelho, Paulo. *The Alchemist*. San Francisco: HarperSanFrancisco, 1993.

Covey, Stephen R., PhD. "Habit 2: Begin with the End in Mind."
https://www.franklincovey.com/the-7-habits/habit-2.html.

Swafford, Jan. *Charles Ives: A Life with Music*. New York: W.W. Norton, 1996.

Whitman, Walt. "Oh Me! Oh Life!" *Leaves of Grass*, 1891. Quoted in Peter Weir, et al., *Dead Poets Society*. Burbank, CA: Touchstone Home Video, 1998.

CHAPTER 2
Eberle, Stephanie K. "A Marathon, Not a Sprint." *Inside Higher Ed*. November 26, 2018. https://www.insidehighered.com/advice/2018/11/26/students-must-start-thinking-about-career-development-early-opinion.

Kolko, Jed. "What the Job Market Looks Like for Today's College Graduates." *Harvard Business Review*, May 9, 2019. https://hbr.org/2019/05/what-the-job-market-looks-like-for-todays-college-graduates.

Leman, Kevin, and William Pentak. *The Way of the Shepherd: 7 Ancient Secrets to Managing Productive People*. Grand Rapids, MI: Zondervan, 2004.

CHAPTER 3
"About Us: We Can Help with Your Small Business Payroll Needs." *SurePayroll*. https://www.surepayroll.com/about.

Alter, Michael. "Embracing Your Fear." Lecture Presented in Entrepreneurial Selling Course of the University of Chicago Booth School of Business, Hyde Park, IL, October 2017.

Divon, Michelle. "Barred from Chocolate for 5 Years, Max Brenner Founder Makes a Sweet Comeback." *The Times of Israel*, August 12, 2018. https://www.timesofisrael.com/barred-from-chocolate-for-5-years-max-brenner-founder-makes-sweet-comeback/.

Gladwell, Malcolm. *Outliers: The Story of Success*. New York: Little, Brown and Company, 2008.

Horn, Joshua. "Shackleton's Ad – Men Wanted for Hazardous Journey." *Discerning History*, May 15, 2013. http://discerninghistory.com/2013/05/shackletons-ad-men-wanted-for-hazerdous-journey/.

Hoy, Amy. "The Fine Art of 'Flinstoning.'" *Stacking the Bricks*. February 8, 2020. https://stackingthebricks.com/the-fine-art-of-flintstoning/.

"Learning at the Edge: Notes & Review." *Vialogue*, January 23, 2012. https://vialogue.wordpress.com/2012/01/23/leading-at-the-edge-notes-review/.

"Never Give Up, Don't Be Afraid to Lead." *The Irish Times*, August 23, 1999. https://www.irishtimes.com/business/never-give-up-don-t-be-afraid-to-lead-1.219497.

"Paychex Completes Acquisition of SurePayroll." *BusinessWire*, February 9, 2011. https://www.businesswire.com/news/home/20110209006290/en/Paychex-Completes-Acquisition-SurePayroll.

Perkins, Dennis, Marget Holtman, and Jillian B. Murphy. *Leading at the Edge: Leadership Lessons from the Extraordinary Saga of Shackleton's Antarctic Expedition*. New York: American Management Association, 2012.

CHAPTER 4

Catmull, Ed. *Creativity Inc.: Overcoming the Unseen Forces That Stand in the Way of True Inspiration*. New York: Random House, 2014. Kindle.

Gerstner Jr., Louis V. *Who Says Elephants Can't Dance?* New York: HarperBusiness, 2002. iBooks.

Graham, Katharine. *Personal History*. New York: Vintage Books, 1998. Audible.

CHAPTER 5

Bell, Chris. "Pixar's Ed Catmull: Interview." *The Telegraph*, April 5, 2014. https://www.telegraph.co.uk/culture/pixar/10719241/Pixars-Ed-Catmull-interview.html.

Catmull, Ed, and Amy Wallace. *Creativity Inc.: Overcoming the Unseen Forces That Stand in the Way of True Inspiration*. New York: Random House, 2014. Kindle.

Davis, Harry. "Competitive Advantage." Lecture Presented in Business Policy Course at the University of Chicago Booth School of Business, Hyde Park, IL, January 2019.

Davis, Harry. "Keynote Speaker." Convocation Address at the University of Chicago Executive MBA Graduation, Hyde Park, IL, April 12, 2019.

"Harry L. Davis." Faculty & Research, Chicago Booth.

"How the World's First Executive MBA Program Changed Business Education." *Chicago Booth Media Relations and Communications*, February 16, 2018. https://news.chicagobooth.edu/newsroom/how-worlds-first-executive-mba-program-changed-business-education.

"Michelle Obama Biography." *Biography*. https://www.biography.com/us-first-lady/michelle-obama.

Obama, Michelle. *Becoming*. New York: Crown, 2018. Kindle.

"Staying One Step Ahead at Pixar: An Interview with Ed Catmull." *McKinsey & Company*, March 2016.
https://www.mckinsey.com/business-functions/organization/our-insights/staying-one-step-ahead-at-pixar-an-interview-with-ed-catmull.

Strauss, Valerie. "What Michelle Obama Told High School Students." *The Washington Post*, November 14, 2013.

CHAPTER 6

Catmull, Ed, and Amy Wallace. *Creativity Inc.: Overcoming the Unseen Forces That Stand in the Way of True Inspiration*. New York: Random House, 2014. Kindle.

Corkindale, Gill. "Overcoming Imposter Syndrome." *Harvard Business Review*, May 7, 2008.
https://hbr.org/2008/05/overcoming-imposter-syndrome.

Ghadiyali, Zainab. "The Secrets to Designing a Curiosity-Driven Career." *First Round Review*.
https://firstround.com/review/the-secrets-to-designing-a-curiosity-driven-career/.

Ibarra, Herminia. "The Authenticity Paradox." *Harvard Business Review*, January–February 2015.

CHAPTER 7

Catmull, Ed, and Amy Wallace. *Creativity Inc.: Overcoming the Unseen Forces That Stand in the Way of True Inspiration*. New York: Random House, 2014. Kindle.

Davis, Harry. "Competitive Advantage." Lecture Presented in Business Policy Course at the University of Chicago Booth School of Business, Hyde Park, IL, January 2019.

"The Design Sprint." *Sprint*.
https://www.thesprintbook.com/how.

Gerstner Jr., Louis V. *Who Says Elephants Can't Dance?* New York: HarperBusiness, 2002. iBooks.

Knapp, Jake, and John Zeratsky. *Make Time: How to Focus on What Matters Every Day*. New York: Penguin Random House, 2018.

Zimmermann, Bernd. "5 Common Mistakes of Change Leadership." *LinkedIn*. March 30, 2019.
https://www.linkedin.com/pulse/5-common-mistakes-change-leadership-bernd-zimmermann/.

CHAPTER 8

TheBestNotes Staff. "TheBestNotes on *The Little Prince* Study Guide." *TheBestNotes.com*, August 20, 2019.
http://thebestnotes.com/booknotes/Little_Prince_Exupery/The_Little_Prince_Study_Guide13.html.

Catmull, Ed, and Amy Wallace. *Creativity Inc.: Overcoming the Unseen Forces That Stand in the Way of True Inspiration*. New York: Random House, 2014. Kindle.

Davis, Harry. "Competitive Advantage." Lecture Presented in Business Policy Course at the University of Chicago Booth School of Business, Hyde Park, IL, January 2019.

Davis, Harry L. "Leadership as Performance Art." PowerPoint Presentation Presented at IT Leadership Conference at University of Chicago Graduate School of Business, 2008. http://www.morassociates.com/2008conf/HarryDavisITLeadershippdf.pdf.

Quinn, Robert E. "Moments of Greatness: Entering the Fundamental State of Leadership." *Harvard Business Review*, July–August 2005. https://hbr.org/2005/07/moments-of-greatness-entering-the-fundamental-state-of-leadership.

Saint-Exupéry, Antoine de. *The Little Prince*. Trans. Katherine Woods. New York: Harcourt Brace & Co., 1943.

CHAPTER 9

"196 – Drew Dudley: Found & Chief Catalyst of Nuance Leadership Inc." *Dose of Leadership*. https://www.doseofleadership.com/drew-dudley/.

Burt, Ron. "Brokerage." Lecture Presented in Strategic Leadership in Management Networks Course at the University of Chicago Booth School of Business, Hyde Park, IL, January 2019.

Catmull, Ed, and Amy Wallace. *Creativity Inc.: Overcoming the Unseen Forces That Stand in the Way of True Inspiration*. New York: Random House, 2014. Kindle.

Constable, Giff. *Talking to Humans: Success Starts with Understanding Your Customers*, 2014.

David, Harry. Business Policy. University of Chicago Booth School of Business, Hyde Park, IL, February 2019.

Davis, Harry. "Learning from Experience/Doing the 'Right' Thing." Lecture Presented in Business Policy Course at the University of Chicago Booth School of Business, Hyde Park, IL, March 2019.

Dr. Lynda. "The Power of Giving People a 'Lollipop Moment.'" *Ever Widening Circles*. https://everwideningcircles.com/2018/02/18/the-power-of-giving-people-a-lollipop-moment/.

Leonhardt, David. "You're Too Busy. You Need a 'Shultz Hour.'" *The New York Times*, April 18, 2017.

Rosoff, Matt. "The Only Reason the Mac Looks Like It Does Is Because Steve Jobs Dropped In on a Course Taught by This Former Monk." *Business Insider*, March 8, 2016. https://www.businessinsider.com/robert-palladino-calligraphy-class-inspired-steve-jobs-2016-3.

Sturm, Mike. "The Shultz Hour: How 60 Minutes Per Week Can Yield Tremendous Returns." *Better Humans*, February 13, 2018. https://medium.com/better-humans/the-shultz-hour-how-60-minutes-per-week-can-yield-tremendous-returns-all-week-7efa96d87103.

"TEDxToronto – Drew Dudley 'Leading with Lollipops,'" TedxTalks. *YouTube*, October 7, 2010. https://www.youtube.com/watch?v=hVCBrkrFrBE.

CHAPTER 10

Dalio, Ray. *Principles: Life and Work*. New York: Simon & Schuster, 2017.

Wallstreet. Directed by Oliver Stone. 20th Century Fox, 2000, DVD.

CHAPTER 11

Catmull, Ed, and Amy Wallace. *Creativity Inc.: Overcoming the Unseen Forces That Stand in the Way of True Inspiration*. New York: Random House, 2014. Kindle.

Davis, Harry. "Creativity." Lecture Presented in Business Policy Course at the University of Chicago Booth School of Business, Hyde Park, IL, January 2019.

CHAPTER 12

"Passion." *Online Etymology Dictionary*. https://www.etymonline.com/word/passion.

www.ingramcontent.com/pod-product-compliance
Lightning Source LLC
LaVergne TN
LVHW011827060526
838200LV00053B/3924